THE LADDER TO SUCCESS IN TRULY LOVING ALLAH

THE LADDER TO SUCCESS IN TRULY LOVING ALLAH

Sullam al-tawfīq ilā maḥabbati Llāhi ʿalā al-taḥqīq

ʿAbd Allāh bin Ḥusayn bin Ṭāhir
BāʿAlawī al-Ḥaḍramī al-Shāfiʿī

Translation & notes by

MUSA FURBER

The Ladder to Success in Truly Loving Allah

Last updated: 17 August 2020

ISBN 978-1-944904-19-7 (paper)

Published by:
Islamosaic
islamosaic.com
publications@islamosaic.com

Cover image licensed by Ingram Image

بسم الله الرحمن الرحيم

All praise is to Allah alone, the Lord of the Worlds
And may He send His benedictions upon
our master Muhammad, his Kin
and his Companions
and grant them
peace

TRANSLITERATION KEY

ء	’ (A distinctive glottal stop made at the bottom of the throat.)
ا	ā, a
ب	b
ت	t
ث	th (Pronounced like the *th* in *think.*)
ج	j
ح	ḥ (A hard *h* sound made at the Adam’s apple in the middle of the throat.)
خ	kh (Pronounced like *ch* in Scottish *loch.*)
د	d
ذ	dh (Pronounced like *th* in *this.*)
ر	r (A slightly trilled *r* made behind the upper front teeth.)
ز	z
س	s
ش	sh
ص	ṣ (An emphatic *s* pronounced behind the upper front teeth.)
ض	ḍ (An emphatic *d*-like sound made by pressing the entire tongue against the upper palate.)
ط	ṭ (An emphatic *t* sound produced behind the front teeth.)
ظ	ẓ (An emphatic *th* sound, like the *th* in *this,* made behind the front teeth.)
ع	‘ (A distinctive Semitic sound made in the middle of the throat and sounding to a Western ear more like a vowel than a consonant.)
غ	gh (A guttural sound made at the top of the throat, resembling the untrilled German and French *r.*)
ف	f
ق	q (A hard *k* sound produced at the back of the palate.)
ك	k
ل	l
م	m
ن	n
ه	h (This sound is like the English *h* but has more body. It is made at the very bottom of the throat and pronounced at the beginning, middle, and ends of words.)
و	ū, u
ي	ī, i, y
ﷺ	A supplication made after mention of the Prophet Muhammad, translated as “May Allah bless him and grant him peace.”

CONTENTS

المُحْتَوَيَاتُ

TRANSLITERATION KEY VI

PREFACE IX

Author's Introduction 1

1 Creed 3

2 Purification and Prayer 34

3 Zakat 62

4 Fasting 69

5 Hajj 74

6 Transactions 79

7 Purification of the Self 89

8 Clarifying Acts of Disobedience 97

Author's Closing Remarks 130

BIBLIOGRAPHY 132

DETAILED TABLE OF CONTENTS 134

PREFACE

المُقَدِّمَةُ

In the Name of Allah, Most Merciful and Compassionate

This booklet contains a translation of *Sullam al-tawfīq ilā maḥabbati Llāhi ʿalā al-taḥqīq* ("*The Ladder of Success to Truly Loving Allah*") by Shaykh ʿAbd Allāh bin Ḥusayn bin Ṭāhir Bāʿ Alawī al-Ḥaḍramī al-Shāfiʿī (1191–1272 AH/1777–1855 CE), a short treatise covering what every Muslim needs to know and practice. These essentials include matters related to creed, rituals, basic transactions and financial responsibilities, purification of the soul, good character, sins that one must avoid and the consequences for committing them.

This range of topics is similar to *Safīnat al-najā* ("*Ark of Salvation*") and *Al-Risālah al-jāmiʿah* ("*The Encompassing Epistle*"). While there are many similarities between these three books, there are also many significant differences.

Readers who have read *Safīnat al-najā* will find that *Sullam al-tawfīq* covers a wider range of issues (e.g., Hajj, basic financial matters, purification of the soul, sins, and repentance) in greater detail and depth. Nonetheless, there are sections where *Safīnat al-najā* is more detailed, most notably where it enumerates the doubled-letters of *Al-Fātiḥah* and the *tashahhud*.

Readers familiar with *Al-Risālah al-jāmiʿah* will notice that *Sullam al-tawfīq* has a similar structure and order (beliefs, worship, purification of the soul, sins), though it covers more issues (e.g., financial matters) and tends to cover everything in greater depth.

Additionally, readers will observe the author introducing material related to an issue that fiqh books tend to gather together in their own separate chapters. For example, when mentioning unlawful acts, he often mentions their associated punishment. So while the book's purpose does not merit having a chapter dedicated to punishments, the author's style prepares the student so that these concepts will already be familiar when he takes the next step and reads a basic primer (like *Ghāyat al-taqrīb*).

I based my translation on Sibṭ al-Jīlānī's edition of the book (Beirut: Sibṭ al-Jīlānī, 1434 AH/2013 CE)—including his clearly-identified additions to the basic text. His additions address most of the things that would have required pulling in material from other sources, like Shaykh Muḥammad bin ʿUmar bin Nawawī al-Jāwī's (–1316 AH) commentary *Mirqāt ṣuʿūd al-taṣdīq*. At one point, I started adding useful material from Shaykh al-Jāwī's commentary. But I soon realized that it contains so much good material that continuing down that path would have required translating all of his book—not the present booklet. I did refer to his commentary while revising the translation and to clarify a few points. The book is also published as chapter 13 of an anthology of the author's works titled *Majmūʿ al-Ḥabīb ʿAbd Allāh bin Ḥusayn bin Ṭāhir BāʿAlawī* (Beirut: Dār al-Ḥāwī, 1429 CE/2008 AH), pp263–287.

Sibṭ al-Jīlānī's edition includes short comments within the basic text, as well as more extensive footnotes. I have translated all of his brief comments, but not his footnotes. Instead, where more commentary is needed, I have drawn it from Shaykh al-Jāwī's commentary. In order to clearly and economically identify the sources of these comments—as well as my own insertions—I have wrapped each source in its own set of braces.

BRACES	SOURCE OF CONTENTS
‹...›	Sibṭ al-Jīlānī's edition
«...»	Al-Jāwī's *Mirqāt ṣuʿūd al-taṣdīq*
[...]	The translator

The reader can ignore the different types of braces unless he is curious about a comment's origin. The translation follows Sibṭ al-Jīlānī's chapter and section titles, but without any braces to indicate their source.

In order to maximize the benefits of this book, I recommend reading *Safīnat al-najā* ("*Ark of Salvation*") first and then *Al-Risālah al-jāmiʿah* ("*The Encompassing Epistle*") after it, as this sequence would gradually expose the reader to an increasing range of topics explored in progressive depth.

If a reader must choose between *Safīnah, Risālah,* or *Sullam*; I recommend *Sullam* for its greater depth and breadth. Readers interested in more details on legal issues will find them in *The Accessible Conspectus* (Islamosaic, 2015). When possible, these texts should be read with an instructor.

I would like to thank the individuals who offered support for this project. I would also like to thank Anaz Zubair, Masood Yusuf, and Mariam Bashar for agreeing to read through an early draft of the book, and Asif Butt for his help with the cover.

Where I have succeeded, it is only through the grace of Allah. Where I have faltered, it is from my own shortcomings. May Allah forgive the author, everyone mentioned in the book, its owners, readers, listeners, and all Muslims—living and dead.

MUSA FURBER

PUTRAJAYA

JULY 13, 2020

AUTHOR'S INTRODUCTION

مُقَدِّمَةُ المُؤَلِّف

الحَمْدُ للهِ رَبِّ العالَمِينَ ،وأشْهَدُ أنْ لا إلٰهَ إلّا اللهُ وَحْدَهُ لا شَرِيكَ لَهُ، وأشْهَدُ أنَّ سَيِّدَنا مُحَمَّدًا عَبْدُهُ ورَسُولُهُ، صَلَّى اللهُ عليه وسَلَّمَ وعلى آلِهِ وصَحْبِهِ والتّابِعِين.

أمّا بَعْدُ، فَهٰذا جُزْءٌ لَطِيفٌ يَسَّرَهُ اللهُ تَعالَى، فِيما يَجِبُ تَعَلُّمُهُ، وتَعْلِيمُهُ، والعَمَلُ بِهِ لِلخاصِّ والعامِّ، والواجِبُ ما وَعَدَ اللهُ فاعِلَهُ بِالثَّوابِ، وتَوَعَّدَ تارِكَهُ بِالعِقابِ، وسَمَّيْتُهُ «سُلَّمَ التَّوْفِيقِ إلى مَحَبَّةِ اللهِ على التَّحْقِيقِ»، أسألُ اللهَ الكَرِيمَ أنْ يَجْعَلَ ذلك مِنْهُ ولَهُ وفِيهِ وإلَيْهِ، ومُوجِبًا لِلقُرْبِ والزُّلْفَى لَدَيْه، وأنْ يُوَفِّقَ مَنْ وَقَفَ عليه لِلْعَمَلِ بِمُقْتَضاه، ثُمَّ التَّرَقِّي بِالتَّوَدُّدِ بِالنَّوافِلِ لِيَحُوزَ حُبَّهُ ووَلاه.

All praise is for Allah, Lord of the Worlds. I testify that there is no deity except Allah, alone and without partner. I testify that our master Muḥammad is His servant and His messenger. May Allah bless him and grant him peace—and his household, his companions, and those who followed them.

To commence: This small monograph (may Allah Most High make it easy!) concerns what is obligatory to teach, learn, and for the specialist and commoner to act upon. (An obligation is that for which Allah promised rewards to those who perform it and threatened punishment to those who neglect to perform it.) I named it *Sullam al-tawfīq ilā maḥabbati Allahi ʿāla al-taḥqīq*. I ask Allah, the Generous, to make it from Him, for Him, in «loving» Him, and to Him—and that warrants nearness and closeness to Him, and [I ask

Him] to grant success to whomever becomes acquainted with it to act upon its necessities, and then, lovingly, progress through voluntary works to obtain His love and friendship.

1

CREED

بَابُ أُصُولِ الدِّينِ

WHAT IS REQUIRED OF EVERY RESPONSIBLE INDIVIDUAL

فَصْلٌ ‹في الواجِبِ على كُلِّ مُكَلَّفٍ›

يَجِبُ على كافَّةِ المُكَلَّفِينَ ‹غَيْرِ المُسْلِمِينَ› الدُّخُولُ في دِينِ الإسْلامِ، والثُّبُوتُ فيه على الدَّوام، والْتِزامُ ما لَزِمَ عليه مِنَ الأحْكام.

All responsible individuals ‹who are not Muslims› are required to enter Islam, remain in it continuously, and adhere to whatever rulings are prescribed for him.

MEANING OF THE TESTIFICATIONS OF FAITH

‹فَصْلٌ: في مَعْنَى الشَّهادَتَيْنِ›

فَمِمّا يَجِبُ عِلْمُهُ واعْتِقادُهُ مُطْلَقًا، والنُّطْقُ به في الحالِ إنْ كانَ كافِرًا، وإلّا ففي الصَّلاةِ، الشَّهادَتانِ وهُما: «أشْهَدُ أنْ لا إلٰهَ إلّا اللهُ، وأشْهَدُ أنَّ مُحَمَّدًا رَسُولُ اللهِ»، صلى الله عليه وسلم.

Among the things that one is unconditionally required to know, believe, and utter are the two testifications of faith [*al-shahādatayn*]—immediately if he is a disbeliever or, otherwise, during prayer. They are: "I testify that there is no deity except Allah. And I testify that Muḥammad is the Messenger of Allah." (May Allah bless him and grant him peace.)

THE FIRST TESTIFICATION

⟨مَعْنَى الشَّهَادَةِ الأُولَى⟩

وَمَعْنَى «أَشْهَدُ أَنْ لا إِلَهَ إِلَّا اللهُ»: أَنْ تَعْلَمَ وَتَعْتَقِدَ وَتُؤْمِنَ وَتُصَدِّقَ أَنْ لا مَعْبُودَ بِحَقٍّ فِي الوُجُودِ إِلَّا اللهُ، الواحِدُ، الأَحَدُ، الأَوَّلُ، القَدِيمُ، الحَيُّ، القَيُّومُ، الباقِي، الدائِمُ، الخالِقُ، الرَّازِقُ، العالِمُ، القَدِيرُ، الفَعَّالُ لِما يُرِيدُ، ما شاءَ اللهُ كانَ وما لم يَشَأْ لم يَكُنْ، ولا حَوْلَ ولا قُوَّةَ إِلَّا بِاللهِ العَلِيِّ العَظِيمِ،

The meaning of "I testify that there is no deity except Allah" is that you know, are convinced of, believe, and consider it true that nothing in existence is rightfully worshiped except for Allah, the One, the Singular, the First, the Beginning-less, the Living, the Self-subsistent, the Endless, the Everlasting, the Creator, the Provider, the Knowing, the Able, Who does whatever He wills. Whatever Allah wishes, is; whatever He wishes not to be, is not. There is no change or power except through Allah, the High and Mighty.

مَوْصُوفٌ بِكُلِّ كَمالٍ، مُنَزَّهٌ عن كُلِّ نَقْصٍ، ﴿لَيْسَ كَمِثْلِهِ شَيْءٌ وَهُوَ السَّمِيعُ البَصِيرُ﴾، فهو القَدِيمُ وما سِواهُ حادِثٌ، وهو الخالِقُ وما سِواهُ مَخْلُوقٌ، وكَلامُهُ قَدِيمٌ ⟨أي بِلا ابْتِداءٍ⟩ كَسائِرِ صِفاتِهِ، لِأَنَّهُ سُبْحانَهُ مُبايِنٌ لِجَمِيعِ المَخْلُوقاتِ فِي الذَّاتِ والصِّفاتِ والأَفْعالِ، ⟨ومَهْما تَصَوَّرْتَ بِبالِك، فَاللهُ تَعالَى لا يُشْبِهُ ذلِك،⟩ سُبْحانَهُ وتَعالَى عَمَّا يَقُولُ الظَّالِمُونَ عُلُوًّا كَبِيرًا.

He is described with every perfection and declared unblemished by any deficiency. "There is nothing like Him; and He is the Hearing, the Seeing" (Q42:11). He is beginning-less and everything else is preceded by non-existence. He is the Creator and everything else is created. His speech is existent from eternity ⟨i.e., without a beginning⟩ like all of His attributes, since He—Glorified is He!—is contrary to all created beings in His essence, attributes, and actions. ⟨Whatever conception you have in your mind, Allah Most High does not resemble that.› Glorified is He and greatly elevated is He from what the wrong-doers say.

THE SECOND TESTIFICATION

‹مَعْنَى الشَّهادَةِ الثَّانِيَةِ›

وَمَعْنَى «أَشْهَدُ أَنَّ مُحَمَّدًا رَسُولُ اللهِ»: أَنْ تَعْلَمَ وَتَعْتَقِدَ وَتُصَدِّقَ وَتُؤْمِنَ أَنَّ سَيِّدَنا وَنَبِيَّنا مُحَمَّدَ بْنَ عَبْدِ اللهِ بْنِ عَبْدِ المُطَّلِبِ بْنِ هاشِمِ بْنِ عَبْدِ مَنافٍ القُرَشِيَّ صَلَّى اللهُ عليه وسَلَّمَ عَبْدُ اللهِ وَرَسُولُهُ إلى جَمِيعِ الخَلْقِ؛ وُلِدَ بِمَكَّةَ، وَبُعِثَ بِها، وهاجَرَ إلى المَدِينَةِ، وَدُفِنَ فيها، وَأَنَّهُ صَلَّى اللهُ عليه وسَلَّمَ صادِقٌ في جَمِيعِ ما أَخْبَرَ بِهِ ‹ومنه السَّمْعِيّاتِ الَّتِي لا تُعْرَفُ بِمُجَرَّدِ العَقْلِ›.

The meaning of "I testify that Muḥammad is the Messenger of Allah" is that you know, are convinced of, believe in, and consider it true that our master and prophet Muḥammad bin ʿAbd Allāh bin ʿAbd al-Muṭṭalib bin Hāshim bin ʿAbd Manāf al-Qurashī (may Allah bless him and grant him peace) is the servant of Allah and His messenger to all of creation. [That] he was born in Mecca and was sent ‹[as a prophet] therein; he emigrated to Medina and was buried there. And that he (May Allah bless him and grant him peace) is truthful in everything he reported ‹including divine disclosures that cannot be known through pure reason›.

OBLIGATORY TO BELIEVE IN DIVINE DISCLOSURES

‹فَصْلٌ فيما يَجِبُ الإيمانُ به مِنَ السَّمْعِيّاتِ›

فَمِنْ ذلك عَذابُ القَبْرِ، وَنَعِيمُهُ، وَسُؤالُ المَلَكَيْنِ مُنْكَرٍ وَنَكِيرٍ، وَالبَعْثُ، وَالحَشْرُ، وَالقِيامَةُ، وَالحِسابُ، وَالثَّوابُ، وَالعَذابُ، وَالمِيزانُ، وَالنَّارُ، وَالصِّراطُ، وَالحَوْضُ، وَالشَّفاعَةُ، وَالجَنَّةُ، وَالخُلُودُ،

These [divine disclosures] include the punishment of the grave and its bliss, the questioning of the two angels (Munkir and Nakīr), the resurrection, the gathering [while waiting for judgment], the turmoil [from the second blowing of the horn until we enter Paradise or the Fire], the accounting, the rewarding, the punishment, the scale, the fire, the bridge, the watering trough, the intercession [in its various forms], paradise, and eternal life [in Paradise for anyone who died a believer, or the Fire for anyone who died a disbeliever].

والرُّؤْيَةُ للهِ سُبْحانَهُ وتَعالَى ‹لا كَما يُرَى المَخْلُوقُ، فَيَراهُ المُؤْمِنُونَ في الآخِرَةِ وهُمْ› في الجَنَّةِ ‹وقَبْلَ دُخُولِها›،

وأَنْ تُؤمِنَ بِمَلائِكَةِ اللهِ، ورُسُلِهِ، وكُتُبِهِ، وبِالقَدَرِ خَيْرِهِ وشَرِّهِ، وأَنَّهُ صَلَّى اللهُ عليه وسَلَّمَ خاتَمُ النَّبِيِّينَ وسَيِّدُ ولَدِ آدَمَ أَجْمَعِينَ.

[They include] seeing Allah, Glorified and Most High is He ‹not as created beings are seen. Believers will see Him› in paradise ‹and before entering it›.

[They include] believing in Allah's angels, His messengers, His books, in destiny—good and bad, and that he (may Allah bless him and grant him peace) is the seal of the Prophets and the chief of all of Adam's children.

SUMMARY OF KNOWING ALLAH MOST HIGH

‹فَصْلٌ في خُلاصَةِ مَعْرِفَةِ اللهِ تعالَى›

‹خُلاصَةُ ما تَقَدَّمَ في مَعْنَى الشَّهادَةِ الأُولَى إِثْباتُ ثَلاثَ عَشْرَةَ صِفَةً للهِ تَعالَى، أي اعْتِقادُ أَنَّها مِنْ صِفاتِهِ تَعالَى الَّتِي لا حَدَّ لَها في العَدِّ، ولا يُحْصِيها أَحَدٌ مِنَ الخَلْقِ، وفَلِلَّهِ تَعالى الكَمالُ المُطْلَقُ غَيْرُ المَحْدُودِ.

‹The summary of what preceded concerning the meaning of the first testification of faith is affirming thirteen attributes to Allah

Most High, meaning: believing that they are among the attributes of Allah that are innumerable and which none of the creation can encompass. For Allah Most High possesses complete perfection without any limitation.

وهذه الصِّفاتُ الثّلاثَةَ عَشَرَ دَلَّ الدَّلِيلُ العَقْليُّ على وُجُوبِها للهِ تَعالَى، وتَكَرَّرَ ذِكْرُها كَثِيرًا في القُرْآنِ والحَدِيثِ، إمّا لَفْظًا وإمّا مَعْنًى؛ فَقالَ العُلَماءُ إنَّه يَجِبُ مَعْرِفَتُها على كُلِّ مُكَلَّفٍ وُجُوبًا عَيْنِيًّا،

These thirteen attributes are shown through rational proofs to be necessary to Allah Most High.[1] They are mentioned frequently in the Quran and hadiths, in phrase or meaning. The scholars said that every responsible individual is specifically required to know them.

وَلَيْسَ مُرَادُهُم مَعرِفَةَ إحاطَةٍ بِحَقائِقِه، بل معرفة محدود تناسب قدرة المخلوق المحدودة؛ فَالخَلْقُ جَمِيعًا عاجِزُونَ عن مَعْرِفَةِ حَقِيقَةِ اللهِ تَعالَى وصِفاتِهِ، فَلا يَعْرِفُ اللهَ على الحَقِيقَةِ إلّا اللهُ، وفيما يلي ذكرها.

They do not mean comprehensively knowing His true realities, but rather a limited knowledge that is appropriate to the limited capabilities of creatures. For the entirety of creation is incapable of knowing the true reality of Allah Most High and His attributes. No one truly knows Allah except Allah. And they [the true realities] are stated as follows:

---

1 In this chapter, *necessary, impossible,* and *possible* refer to rational judgments [*aḥkām 'aqliyyah*]. Roughly speaking: the *necessary* [*wājib*] is that which the sound intellect does not accept to be negated or absent in and of itself; the *impossible* [*mustaḥīl*] is that which the sound intellect does not accept to be affirmed or present in and of itself; and the possible [*jā'iz, mumkin*] is that which the sound intellect accepts to be affirmed or negated, and to be present or absent in and of itself.

WHAT IS NECESSARY FOR ALLAH

[ما يَجِبُ لِلَّهِ تعالى]

What is necessary for Allah Most High and is obligatory for us to know [are the following attributes]:

1. existence,
2. unicity,
3. beginning-less-ness,
4. endlessness,
5. absence of resemblance to anything,
6. absolute self-subsistence,
7. ability,
8. will,
9. knowledge,
10. hearing (without ears),
11. sight (without eyes),
12. life (without a spirit),
13. speech (without letters, sounds, and language).

ما يَجِبُ لِلَّهِ تعالى وَيَجِبُ عَلَيْنَا مَعْرِفَتُهُ:

١. صِفَةُ الوُجُودِ
٢. وصِفَةُ الوَحْدانِيَّةِ
٣. وصِفَةُ الأَزَلِيَّةِ
٤. وصِفَةُ البَقاءِ
٥. وصِفَةُ عَدَمِ مُشابَهَةِ غَيْرِهِ
٦. وصِفَةُ الاسْتِغْناءِ المُطْلَقِ عَنْ غَيْرِهِ
٧. وصِفَةُ القُدْرَةِ
٨. وصِفَةُ الإرادَةِ
٩. وصِفَةُ العِلْمِ
١٠. وصِفَةُ السَّمْعِ (بِلا أُذُنٍ)
١١. وصِفَةُ البَصَرِ (بِلا عَيْنٍ)
١٢. وصِفَةُ الحَياةِ (بِلا رُوحٍ)
١٣. وصِفَةُ الكَلامِ (بِلا حَرْفٍ ولا صَوْتٍ ولا لُغَةٍ).

تنبيهٌ: وصِفاتُ الألُوهِيَّةِ لا تَتَغيَّرُ فَلَيْسَتْ طارِئَةً بَلْ هي صِفاتٌ للهِ بِلا ابْتِداءٍ، لأنَّ صِفاتِ الأَزَلِيِّ لا تَكُونُ إلّا أَزَلِيَّةً، ولا شَبَهَ بَيْنَ صِفاتِ اللهِ وبَيْنَ ما يُسَمَّى بِأَسْمائِها مِنْ صِفاتِ المَخْلُوقاتِ، وإنْ كانَتِ المَعانِي اللُّغَوِيَّةُ لِما يُسَمَّى بِاسْمِها مِنْ صِفاتِ المَخْلُوقاتِ تُقَرِّبُ لِعُقُولِنا فَهْمَ ما يُمْكِنُنا فَهْمُهُ عَنْها، مَعَ اسْتِحْضارِ أَنَّهُ لَيْسَ بَيْنَ صِفاتِ الخَلْقِ وصِفاتِ الحَقِّ اشْتِراكٌ أَصْلًا ولا مُشابَهَةٌ بَتاتًا.

‹Note. The divine attributes do not change. They did not happen. Rather, they are attributes of Allah without beginning since the attributes of the beginning-less are beginning-less. There is no resemblance between the attributes of Allah and the attributes of creatures with the same names—though the linguistic meanings of the attributes of created entities given their names do make it easier for our intellect to understand whatever it is capable of understanding of those attributes—while bearing in mind that between the attributes of creatures and the attributes of the True [Allah] there is no commonality to begin with or resemblance at all.›

وحُكْمُ العَقْلِ بِوُجُوبِ هذِهِ الصِّفاتِ المَذْكُورَةِ للهِ تَعالَى يَعْنِي أَنَّ العَقْلَ لا يَقْبَلُ ولا يُصَدِّقُ أَنْ يَكُونَ اللهُ مُتَّصِفًا بِأَضْدادِها، أي أَنَّ العَقْلَ يَحْكُمُ أَيْضًا بِاسْتِحالَةِ صِفاتِ النَّقْصِ الَّتِي تُقابِلُها وتُنافِيها عليه تَعالَى، ويَنْفِيها قَطْعًا عنه تَعالَى، وكذلك النَّقْلُ يَدُلُّ على انْتِفائِها عنه تَعالَى.

‹The rational mind's judgment of these aforementioned attributes being necessary for Allah Most High means that the rational mind does not accept and does not conceive of Allah being described with their opposites, i.e., the rational mind also judges the attributes of deficiency which are opposite to them and are inconsistent with Allah Most High to be impossible, and it [the rational mind] negates them from Him with certainty. Similarly, transmitted knowledge proves that they are negated from Him Most High.›

WHAT IS IMPOSSIBLE FOR ALLAH

‹What is impossible for Allah and is obligatory for us to know:

1. non-existence,
2. multiplicity,
3. origination,
4. termination,
5. resemblance,
6. need,
7. inability,
8. being compelled or lacking volition,
9. ignorance,
10. deafness,
11. blindness,
12. death, and
13. muteness (in the meaning of negating the attribute of beginningless speech that is without language and sound from Him).›

[ما يَسْتَحِيلُ على اللَّهِ تعالى]

ما يَسْتَحِيلُ على اللَّهِ تَعالَى ويحب علينا معرفته:

١. العَدَمُ
٢. والتَّعَدُّدُ
٣. والابْتِداءُ
٤. والانْتِهاءُ
٥. ومُشابَهَةُ غَيْرِهِ
٦. والاحْتِياجُ إلى غَيْرِهِ
٧. والعَجْزُ عن شَيْءٍ
٨. وأنْ يَكُونَ مُكْرَها على أمْرٍ، أو بِلا اخْتِيارٍ في فِعْلٍ
٩. والجَهْلُ بِشَيْءٍ
١٠. والصَّمَمُ
١١. والعَمَى
١٢. والمَوْتُ
١٣. والبَكَمُ (بِمَعْنَى انْتِفاءِ صِفَةِ الكَلامِ الأزَلِيِّ الذي لَيْسَ بِلُغَةٍ وصَوْتٍ عنه تَعالَى).

CREED

‹مَا يَجُوزُ فِي حَقِّ اللهِ تَعَالَى وَيَجِبُ عَلَيْنَا مَعْرِفَتَهُ: وَدَلَّ العَقْلُ والنَّقْلُ أَيْضًا عَلَى أَنَّهُ يَجُوزُ أَنْ يُوجِدَ اللهُ أَيَّ مُمْكِنٍ أَوْ يَتْرُكَ إِيجَادَهُ، وَلٰكِنَّهُ تَعَالَىٰ لَا يُوجِدُ إِلَّا مَا سَبَقَ فِي عِلْمِهِ الأَزَلِيِّ وَمَشِيئَتِهِ الأَزَلِيَّةِ أَنَّهُ يَدْخُلُ فِي الوُجُودِ، فَيُوجِدُ اللهُ تَعَالَى المَخْلُوقَ فِي وَقْتِهِ عَلَى حَسَبِ مَا عَلِمَهُ اللهُ وَشَاءَهُ بِلَا ابْتِدَاءٍ›.

‹It is possible for Allah and required of us to know—and the rational mind and transmitted knowledge also indicate it—that it is permissible for Allah to bring anything that is rationally possible into existence or to not bring it into existence. But Allah Most High does not bring into existence except what [accords with that which] is already in His beginning-less knowledge and His beginning-less will that it would enter into existence. Thus, Allah Most High brings a creature into existence in its time according to what He knows and wills without origination.›

GENERAL PROOF FOR THE EXISTENCE OF ALLAH AND HIS ATTRIBUTES

‹فَصْلٌ: فِي الدَّلِيلِ الإِجْمَالِيِّ عَلَى وُجُودِ اللهِ وَصِفَاتِهِ›

‹يَجِبُ عَلَى المُكَلَّفِ أَنْ يَعْرِفَ الدَّلِيلَ الإِجْمَالِيَّ عَلَى وُجُودِ اللهِ تَعَالَى وَصِفَاتِهِ لِيُحَصِّنَ إِيمَانَهُ، وَمِثَالُهُ أَنْ يَقُولَ فِي نَفْسِهِ: أَنَا وُجِدْتُ فِي بَطْنِ أُمِّي، بَعْدَ أَنْ لَمْ أَكُنْ مَوْجُودًا، وَمَنْ وُجِدَ بَعْدَ أَنْ لَمْ يَكُنْ فَلَا بُدَّ لَهُ مِنْ مُوجِدٍ أَيْ خَالِقٍ أَوْجَدَهُ وَكَوَّنَهُ، فَلَا بُدَّ لِي مِنْ خَالِقٍ خَلَقَ لِي أَعْضَائِيَ وَأَجْزَائِيَ وَتَفَاصِيلِيَ الدَّاخِلِيَّةَ وَالخَارِجِيَّةَ، وَذٰلِكَ المُكَوِّنُ الَّذِي كَوَّنَنِي وَأَوْجَدَنِي لَيْسَ أَبِي وَلَا أُمِّي وَلَا أَيُّ مَخْلُوقٍ آخَرَ، بَلْ هُوَ خَالِقٌ عَظِيمٌ، خَلَقَ كُلَّ مَا فِي هٰذَا الكَوْنِ، وَيُسَيْطِرُ عَلَى كُلِّ ذَرَّةٍ مِنْ ذَرَّاتِهِ سَيْطَرَةً تَامَّةً، فَهُوَ إِلٰهٌ وَاحِدٌ، لَا شَرِيكَ وَلَا مَثِيلَ لَهُ، وَهُوَ مُنَزَّهٌ عَنْ كُلِّ نَقْصٍ، فَلَهُ الكَمَالُ المُطْلَقُ غَيْرُ المَحْدُودِ، فَلَا بُدَّ أَنْ يَكُونَ مُتَّصِفًا

بِالعِلْمِ وَالقُدْرَةِ وَالإِرَادَةِ وَالحَيَاةِ وَسَائِرِ صِفَاتِ الكَمَالِ عَلَى مَا يَلِيقُ بِالأُلُوهِيَّةِ، وَعُقُولُ الخَلْقِ لَا تُحِيطُ بِهِ عِلْمًا، وَيُسَمَّى بِالعَرَبِيَّةِ «اللهَ»›.

‹A responsible individual is required to know the general proof for the existence of Allah Most High and His attributes in order to safeguard his belief. An example of it [i.e., a general proof] is saying to himself: "I came to be in my mother's womb after I did not exist. And what exists after not existing must have something that produces it, meaning a creator who produced and formed it. So there must be a creator who created my limbs and my parts, and my internal and external details. That former who formed me and produced me is not my father, my mother, or any other creature. Rather, it is an immense creator: it created everything that exists in this cosmos and it has complete control over each of its [the cosmos'] atoms. It is a singular deity without partner and peer. It is unblemished by any deficiency. It has absolute perfection without limitation. It must be described with [possessing] knowledge, ability, will, life, and all the other attributes of perfection that fit the divine. The minds of created beings cannot have comprehensive knowledge of it. In Arabic, it is named *Allāh*."›

‹فصل في جَوَابِ مَنْ يَسْأَلُ: «مَا هُوَ اللهُ؟»›

ANSWER TO WHOMEVER ASKS "WHAT IS ALLAH?"

‹مِنَ المُهِمِّ أَنْ يَعْرِفَ المُسْلِمُ كَيْفَ يُجِيبُ مَنْ يَسْأَلُ: «مَا هُوَ اللهُ؟»، فَهَذَا سُؤَالٌ يَطْرَحُهُ كَثِيرٌ مِنَ الصِّغَارِ، وَلَا يُحْسِنُ الإِجَابَةَ عَلَيْهِ كَثِيرٌ مِنَ الكِبَارِ؛ وَيُمْكِنُ إِجَابَتُهُ إِجَابَةً صَحِيحَةً بِأَنْ يُقَالَ:›

‹Among what is important for a Muslim to know is how to answer someone who asks "What is Allah?" This is a question many youngsters ask, yet many elders are not able to properly answer. It is possible to provide a valid answer by saying:›

اللهُ تَعالَى مَوْجُودٌ لا يُشْبِهُ غَيْرَهُ مِنَ المَوْجُوداتِ، فَمَهْما تَصَوَّرْتَ بِبالِكَ فَاللهُ لا يُشْبِهُ ذلك.

ولكن يجدر أن نذكر أننا - بِناءً على الأَدِلَّةِ القَطْعِيَّةِ - نَعْلَمُ يَقِينًا عَنِ اللهِ تَعالَى أُمُورًا مِنْها:

أن الله تعالى حَقِيقَتُهُ لَيْسَتْ كَحَقِيقَةِ أَحَدٍ غَيْرِهِ، فَلَيْسَ تَعالَى مِنْ أَفْرادِ الكَوْنِ أي العالَمِ، ولا يعلم حقيقة الله أحد غيره تعالى؛

‹Allah Most High exists. No other existent resembles Him. Whatever you conceive of in your mind, Allah does not resemble it.

However, we should mention that we—based upon incontrovertible proofs—know some matters about Allah with certainty. Among them are:

That the true reality of Allah Most High is not like the true reality of anything else. Allah Most High is not a member of the cosmos, i.e., the universe. No one knows the true reality of Allah other than He Most High.›

وأَنَّ اللهَ تَعالَى لَيْسَ في أَيِّ مَكانٍ أو جِهَةٍ؛ لِأَنَّهُ لَيْسَ ذا جِسْمٍ وحَجْمٍ وشَكْلٍ؛

وأَنَّ اللهَ تَعالَى لا يَحْتاجُ إِلى شَيْءٍ، ولا يَتَضَرَّرُ بِشَيْءٍ، ولا يَنْتَفِعُ بِشَيْءٍ؛ لِأَنَّ لَهُ الكَمالَ المُطْلَقَ؛

وأَنَّ اللهَ تَعالَى لا بِدايَةَ لِوُجُودِهِ، فَلَيْسَ لَهُ خالِقٌ؛ أَمّا غَيْرُهُ فَلِوُجُودِهِ بِدايَةٌ، فَيَحْتَاجُ إِلى خالِقٍ؛

‹That Allah Most High is not in any location or direction since He does not possess a body, volume, or form.

That Allah Most High is not in need of anything, is not harmed by anything, and is not benefited by anything, since He possesses absolute perfection.›

‹That Allah Most High has no beginning to His existence, so He has no creator. As for others, their existence does have a beginning, so they do need a creator.

وأنَّ اللهَ تَعالَى خالِقُ كُلِّ ما سِواهُ، أي كُلِّ ما في العالَمِ من الأجسام والأعمال وغيرها، فلا خالق سواه؛

وأنَّ اللهَ تَعالَى لا يجب عليه شيء، وليس لأحد حقّ عليه، ولكنّه تعالى وعده حقّ ووعيده صدق؛

وأنَّ كل ما أَوْهَمَتْ ظَواهِرُهُ مِنَ الآياتِ الكَرِيمَةِ والأَحادِيثِ الشَّرِيفَةِ اتِّصافَ اللهِ تَعالَى بِصِفَةٍ مِنْ صِفاتِ المَخْلُوقاتِ، كَالجِسْمِ والمَكانِ والحَرَكَةِ والسُّكُونِ، فَتَفْسِيرُهُ الصَّحِيحُ غَيْرُ ذلك قَطْعًا›.

That Allah Most High is the creator of everything other than Him, i.e., everything in the world, including bodies, actions, and other things. There is no creator except Him.›

‹That nothing is required of Allah Most High. No one holds any right over Him. But He Most High: His promise is true and His threat is true.

Whatever apparent meaning of the noble verses of the Quran and the honorable hadiths might seems to describe Allah Most High with one of the attributes of created beings (like corporeality, place, motion, and stillness)—their valid explanation is, with certainty, something else.›

SUMMARY OF KNOWING THE PROPHETS (BLESSINGS AND PEACE BE UPON THEM)

‹خُلاصَةٌ في مَعْرِفَةِ الأَنْبِياءِ عليهم الصَّلاةُ والسَّلامُ›

‹المُعْجِزاتُ دَلِيلٌ قاطِعٌ على صِدْقِ الأَنْبِياءِ: ويَجِبُ اعْتِقادُ أَنَّ المُعْجِزاتِ دَلِيلٌ يَقِينِيٌّ على صِدْقِ الأَنْبِياءِ، الَّذِينَ هُمْ أَفْضَلُ خَلْقِ اللهِ تَعالَى، وسُفَراؤُهُ إلى غَيْرِهِمْ مِنْ خَلْقِهِ، وهي خَوارِقُ لِلعاداتِ الكَوْنِيَّةِ في الدُّنْيا أَيَّدَهُمُ اللهُ بِها وخَصَّهُمْ بها إظْهارًا لِتَصْدِيقِهِ لَهُمْ، وجَعَلَها مُوافِقَةً لِدَعْواهُمُ النُّبُوَّةَ، وأَعْجَزَ عن الإتْيانِ بِمِثْلِها كُلَّ مُتَنَبِّئٍ زُورًا وكلَّ مُكَذِّبٍ لأَحَدٍ مِنَ الأَنْبِياءِ.

‹Miracles are an incontrovertible proof for the truthfulness of the prophets. It is obligatory to believe that the miracles are a certain proof for the truthfulness of the prophets, who are the most superior of Allah Most High's creation and His ambassadors to others of His creation. Miracles are violations of the natural norms in this world [*al-dunyā*]. Allah assisted them [the prophets] with miracles and singled them out with [miracles] to manifest His attestation of them. He made miracles matching their claims of prophethood, and He rendered incapable any false prophet or anyone who belied any of the Prophets from bringing forth anything like them›

WHAT IS NECESSARY FOR THE PROPHETS

‹What is necessary for the prophets and is obligatory for us to know: It is obligatory to believe that it is necessary—by means of rational proofs, religious proofs, or both together— for each of Allah's prophets (may Allah bless them and give them peace) to have praiseworthy attributes. They include:

1. truthfulness,
2. loyalty,
3. conveyance [of the message],
4. astuteness,
5. preservation (which is being far from anything that would render them defective), and
6. protection from disbelief and all sins—major and minor—before prophethood and afterwards.›

[ما يَجِبُ لِلْأَنْبِياءِ]

ما يَجِبُ لِلْأَنْبِياءِ ويجب علينا معرفته: ويَجِبُ اعْتِقادُ أنَّ كُلَّ نَبِيٍّ مِنْ أنْبِياءِ اللهِ عليهم الصَّلاةُ والسَّلامُ يَجِبُ لَهُ - بالدَّلِيلِ العَقْلِيِّ أو بالدَّلِيلِ الشَّرْعِيِّ أو بِهِما مَعًا - صِفاتٌ حَمِيدَةٌ، منها:

١. الصِّدْقُ،
٢. والأمانَةُ،
٣. والتَّبْلِيغُ،
٤. والفَطانَةُ،
٥. والصِّيانَةُ (وهي البُعْدُ عَمّا يَعِيبُ)،
٦. والعِصْمَةُ مِنَ الكُفْرِ وسائِرِ الذُّنُوبِ كَبِيرِها وصَغِيرِها، قَبْلَ النُّبُوَّةِ وبَعْدَها.

WHAT IS IMPOSSIBLE FOR THE PROPHETS

‹What is impossible for the prophets and obligatory for us to know: The opposites of the attributes required for them are impossible for any of the prophets. Among what is impossible for them is

1. lying,
2. treachery,
3. concealing anything Allah Most High ordered them to convey,
4. lowliness,
5. stupidity,
6. being defeated,
7. baseness,
8. foolishness,
9. disbelief. and
10. whatever has been written about them sinning—before and after prophethood.

[ما يَسْتَحِيلُ على الأَنْبياءِ]

ما يَسْتَحِيلُ على الأَنْبياءِ ويجب علينا معرفته: يَسْتَحِيلُ على أيٍّ مِنَ الأَنْبياءِ أَضْدادُ الصِّفاتِ الواجِبَةِ لَهُمْ، فَمِمّا يَسْتَحِيلُ عَلَيْهِمْ:

١. الكَذِبُ،
٢. والخِيانَةُ،
٣. وكِتْمانُ شَيْءٍ أَمَرَهُمُ اللهُ تَعالَى بِتَبْلِيغِهِ،
٤. والرَّذالَةُ،
٥. والسَّفاهَةُ،
٦. والهَزِيمَةُ،
٧. والخِسَّةُ،
٨. والغَباوَةُ،
٩. والكُفْرُ،
١٠. وما يُكْتَبُ عليهم بِهِ ذَنْبٌ، قَبْلَ النُّبُوَّةِ وبَعْدَها؛

وكُلُّ عِبارَةٍ، مِمّا ثَبَتَ عن اللهِ تَعالَى أو عن رَسُولِهِ صَلَّى اللهُ عليه وسَلَّمَ، إذا أوْهَمَ ظاهِرُها اتصاف أحد من الأنبياء بِشَيءٍ مما يستحيل عليهم، فَتَفْسِيرُها الصَّحِيحُ ومعناها المراد غَيْرُ ظاهِرِها.

Every expression that is established as being from Allah Most High or His Messenger (may Allah bless him and grant him peace)—if its apparent meaning appears to indicate one of the prophets being described with something impossible for them—its valid explanation and intended meaning is other than what is apparent.›

ما يَجُوزُ في حَقِّ الأَنْبياءِ وَيَجِبُ عَلَيْنا مَعْرِفَتَهُ: ويَجِبُ اعْتِقادُ أنَّ جَمِيعَ الأنْبياءِ بَشَرٌ فَيَجُوزُ عليهم الأعْراضُ البَشرِيَّةُ الَّتي لا تُنافِي مَقامَهُمْ ومُهِمَّتَهُمْ وما يَجِبُ لَهُم؛ فَيَجُوزُ عليهم الأَكْلُ، والشُّرْبُ، والزَّواجُ، والمَرَضُ غيرُ المُنَفِّرِ منهم وغيرُ المُخِلِّ بِدَعْوَتِهِمْ، ونَوْمُ العَيْنِ لا القَلْبِ، والمَوْتُ›.

‹What is possible with respect to the prophets and obligatory for us to know: It is required to believe that all of the prophets were humans. So it is possible for them to have human conditions that do not negate their station, their mission, and what is required for them. Thus, it is possible for them to eat, drink, marry, fall sick with a sickness that is not repulsive or undermining to their call, sleep with their eyes (but not their hearts), and die.›

WHAT REMOVES A PERSON FROM ISLAM

فَصْلٌ ‹فِيما يُخرِجُ مِنَ الإِسْلامِ›

يَجِبُ على كُلِّ مُسْلِمٍ حِفْظُ إِسْلامِهِ وصَوْنُهُ عَمّا يُفْسِدُهُ ويُبْطِلُهُ ويَقْطَعُهُ، وهو الرِّدَّةُ ‹أي الكُفْرُ بَعْدَ الإِسْلامِ› والعِياذُ بِاللهِ تَعالَى، وقَدْ كَثُرَ في هذا الزَّمانِ التَّساهُلُ في الكَلامِ حَتَّى إِنَّهُ يَخْرُجُ مِنْ بَعْضِهِمْ أَلْفاظٌ تُخْرِجُهُمْ عن الإِسْلامِ، ولا يَرَوْنَ ذلك ذَنْبًا فَضْلًا عن كَوْنِهِ كُفْرًا.

والرِّدَّةُ ثَلاثَةُ أَقْسامٍ: اعْتِقاداتٌ وأَفْعالٌ وأَقْوالٌ، وكُلُّ قِسْمٍ يَتَشَعَّبُ شُعَبًا كَثِيرَةً.

Every Muslim is required to safeguard his Islam and protect it from what spoils it, invalidates it, and interrupts it—which is apostasy ‹i.e., disbelief after Islam›. May Allah Most High protect us! In this time, there is such tremendous leniency in speech that words are uttered by people that remove them from Islam without them even seeing this as sinful—let alone it being disbelief.

There are three categories of disbelief: beliefs, actions, and statements. Each category has numerous sub-categories.

APOSTASY VIA THE HEART

‹أَمْثِلَةُ الرِّدَّةِ بِالقَلْبِ›

فَمِنَ الأَوَّلِ ‹أي الاعْتِقاداتِ الكُفْرِيَّةِ›:

١. الشَّكُّ في اللهِ، أو في رَسُولِهِ، أو القُرْآنِ، أو اليَوْمِ الآخِرِ، أو الجَنَّةِ، أو النّارِ، أو الثَّوابِ، أو العِقابِ، ونَحْوِ ذلك مِمّا هو مُجمَعٌ عليه ‹مَعْلُومٌ مِنَ الدِّينِ بِالضَّرُورَةِ مِمّا لا يَخْفَى عليه›؛

٢. أو ‹مَنِ› اعتَقَدَ فَقْدَ ‹أي نَفْيَ› صِفَةٍ مِنْ صِفاتِ اللهِ الواجِبَةِ إِجْماعًا ‹مِمّا دَلَّ عليه العَقْلُ› كَالعِلْمِ،

٣. أو ‹مَنْ› نَسَبَ له ‹تَعالَى› صِفَةً يَجِبُ تَنْزِيهُهُ عنها إجْماعًا ‹مِمّا يَدُلُّ العَقْلُ على أَنَّهُ نَقْصٌ في حَقِّهِ تَعالَى›، كَالجِسْمِ،

٤. أو ‹مَنْ› حَلَّلَ مُحَرَّمًا بِالإجْماعِ مَعْلُومًا مِنَ الدِّينِ بِالضَّرُورَةِ مِمّا لا يَخْفَى عليه، كالزِّنا واللِّواطِ والقَتْلِ والسَّرِقَةِ والغَصْبِ ‹أي أَخْذِ أَمْوالِ النّاسِ بِغَيْرِ حَقٍّ قَهْرًا›؛

٥. أو ‹مَنْ› حَرَّمَ حَلالًا كذلك ‹أي مِمّا هو مَعْلُومٌ مِنَ الدِّينِ بِالضَّرُورَةِ مِمّا لا يَخْفَى عليه›، كالبَيْعِ والنِّكاحِ؛

The first ‹i.e., beliefs that result in disbelief› include:

1. Doubt in Allah, His Messenger, the Quran, the Final Day, paradise, fire, reward, punishment, and similar things that are matters of consensus ‹[which are] necessarily known as part of the religion[2] and not [typically] hidden to [common people like] him [lit. "are not hidden to him"]›.
2. [Someone] believing the absence ‹i.e., negation› of a single of Allah's attributes that is, according to consensus, necessary ‹and which is proven through reason›, like knowledge.
3. Ascribing to Him ‹Most High is He› an attribute that, according to consensus, is necessary for Him to be free of ‹and which is proven through reason›, like corporeality.
4. Declaring as lawful that which is unlawful according to consensus and is necessarily known as part of the religion and is not [typically] hidden to [common people like] him, like fornication, anal sex, killing, stealing, taking by force ‹i.e., forcibly taking property from people without right›.
5. Declaring as unlawful that which is lawful in a similar manner ‹i.e., something that is necessarily known as part

2 This phrase refers to things that anyone who is a Muslim typically knows to be part of the religion, whether that individual is knowledgeable or ignorant.

of the religion and is not [typically] hidden to [common people like] him›, like trade and marriage.

٦. أو ‹مَنْ› نَفَى وُجُوبَ مُجْمَعٍ عليه كذلك ‹أي مِمّا هو مَعْلُومٌ مِنَ الدِّينِ بِالضَّرُورَةِ مِمّا لا يَخْفَى عليه›، كَالصَّلَواتِ الخَمْسِ، أو سَجْدَةٍ منها، والزَّكاةِ، والصَّوْمِ، والحَجِّ، والوُضُوءِ؛

٧. أو ‹مَنْ› أَوْجَبَ ما لم يَجِبْ إجْماعًا كذلك ‹أي مِمّا هو مَعْلُومٌ مِنَ الدِّينِ بِالضَّرُورَةِ مِمّا لا يَخْفَى عليه، كَصِيَامِ شَهْرٍ غَيْرَ رَمَضَان›؛

٨. أو ‹مَنْ› نَفَى مَشْرُوعِيَّةَ مُجْمَعٍ عليه كذلك ‹أي مِمّا هو مَعْلُومٌ مِنَ الدِّينِ بِالضَّرُورَةِ مِمّا لا يَخْفَى عليه›، كَالرَّواتِبِ؛

٩. أو ‹مَنْ› عَزَمَ على الكُفْرِ ‹مُطْلَقًا› في المُسْتَقْبَلِ؛

١٠. أو ‹مَنْ عَزَمَ› على فِعْلِ شَيْءٍ ‹معيّن مِنَ الكُفْرِيّاتِ› مِمّا ذُكِرَ ‹أو نَحْوِه› في المُسْتَقْبَلِ، أو تَرَدَّدَ فيه، لا وَسْوَسَةٌ؛

6. Negating an obligation about which there is consensus in a similar manner ‹i.e., something necessarily known as part of the religion which is not [typically] hidden to [common people like] him›, like the five prayers, one of their prostrations, zakat, fasting, Hajj, and ablution.
7. Obligating something that is not obligatory according to consensus in a similar manner ‹i.e., something necessarily known as part of the religion which is not [typically] hidden to [common people like] him, like fasting a month other than Ramadan›.
8. Negating the legitimacy of something that is considered legitimate according to consensus in a similar manner ‹i.e., something necessarily known as part of the religion which is not [typically] hidden to [common people like] him›, like voluntary prayers associated with the obligatory prayers.
9. Being resolved to disbelieve ‹unconditionally› in the future.

10. [Deciding] to perform something ‹[i.e.,] a particular cause of disbelief› of the aforementioned ‹or their like› in the future, or wavering about it—but not [when it is only] evil whisperings.

١١. أو ‹مَنْ› أَنْكَرَ صُحْبَةَ سَيِّدِنا أَبِي بَكْرٍ الصديق رَضِيَ اللهُ عنه ‹أي نفى كونه من صحابة نبينا صلى الله عليه وسلم›؛

١٢. أو ‹مَنْ أَنْكَرَ› رِسالَةَ واحِدٍ مِنَ الرُّسُلِ المُجْمَعِ على رِسالَتِهِ ‹أي مِمَّنْ رِسالَتُهُ مِنَ المَعْلُومِ مِنَ الدِّينِ بِالضَّرُورَةِ الَّذِي لا يَخْفَى عليه، كَسَيِّدِنا عِيسَى وسَيِّدِنا مُوسَى عليهما الصَّلاةُ والسَّلامُ›؛

١٣. أو ‹مَنْ› جَحَدَ حَرْفًا مُجْمَعًا عليه مِنَ القُرْآنِ ‹وهو يَعْتَقِدُ أَنَّهُ منه، أو عنادًا›،

١٤. أو زادَ حَرْفًا فيه مُجْمَعًا على نَفْيِهِ ‹مَعَ كَوْنِهِ› مُعْتَقِدًا أَنَّهُ ‹لَيْسَ› منه ‹أو عنادًا›؛

١٥. أو ‹مَنْ› كَذَّبَ رَسُولًا، أو نَقَّصَهُ،

١٦. أو صَغَّرَ اسْمَهُ بِقَصْدِ تَحْقِيرِهِ؛

١٧. أو ‹مَنْ› جَوَّزَ نُبُوَّةَ أَحَدٍ بَعْدَ نَبِيِّنا مُحَمَّدٍ صَلَّى اللهُ عليه وسَلَّمَ.

11. Denying that our master Abū Bakr al-Ṣiddīq (may Allah be pleased with him) was a companion ‹i.e., negating that he was a companion of our Prophet (may Allah bless him and grant him peace)›.
12. [Denying] the messenger-hood of one of the messengers upon whom there is consensus regarding his messenger-hood ‹i.e., one of those whose messenger-hood is necessarily known as part of the religion which is not [typically] hidden to [common people like] him, like our master ʿĪsā and our master Mūsā (peace and blessings be upon them)›.

13. Renouncing a single letter of the Quran where there is consensus regarding it being part of the Quran ‹while believing that it is part of it, or [renouncing it] out of stubbornness›.
14. Adding a letter [to the Quran] where there is consensus negating it [as being part of the Quran] ‹despite› believing it is ‹not› part of it ‹or out of pigheadedness›.
15. Declaring a messenger a liar or debasing him.
16. Using a diminutive form of a [messenger's] name with the intent of showing contempt.
17. Considering it possible for someone to be a prophet after our Prophet Muḥammad (may Allah bless him and grant him peace).

APOSTASY THROUGH THE LIMBS ‹أَمْثِلَةُ الرِّدَّةِ بِالجَوارِحِ›

والقِسْمُ الثّاني الأفْعالُ ‹الكُفْرِيَّةُ›:

١. كَسُجُودٍ لِصَنَمٍ أو شَمْسٍ ‹أو قَمَرٍ أو شَيْطانٍ مُطْلَقًا›، أو مَخْلُوقٍ آخَرَ ‹على وَجْهِ عِبادَتِهِ›.

‹ومن أمثلة الكفر بفعل الجوارح أيضا:

٢. رمي المصحف، أو كتاب علم شرعيّ، أو اسم الله، أو نحو ذلك من معظمات الشرع، عمدا في القذر، لأنه يدل على الاستهزاء والاستخفاف بالدين.

٣. والوطء عمدًا بالقدم على المصحف ونحوه من معظمات الشرع، ككتب الفقه الإسلامي، لأنه كرميه في القذر يدل على الاستهزاء والاستخفاف بالدين.

٤.   وكتابة ما يكفر المرء بالنطق به، لا على وجه الحكاية عن غيرها›.

The second category are actions ‹that result in disbelief›, such as

1. Prostrating to an idol, the sun ‹or the moon, or Satan—unconditionally›, or to other created beings ‹in the manner of worshiping it›.

‹Also from among the examples of disbelief through acts of the body are:

2. Throwing the Quran, a book of religious knowledge, the name "*Allāh*," or something similar that the Sacred Law reveres into something dirty since it indicates mockery of and contempt for the religion.
3. Deliberately stepping on the Quran or something similar that the Sacred Law reveres (like books of Islamic law) since it is similar to throwing them in filth in indicating mockery of and contempt for the religion.
4. Writing an utterance that results in disbelief—though not when quoting someone else.›

APOSTASY THROUGH THE TONGUE ‹أمْثِلَةُ الرِّدَّةِ بِاللِّسانِ›

والقِسْمُ الثّالِثُ الأقْوالُ ‹الكُفْرِيَّةُ›، وهي كَثِيرَةٌ جِدًّا لا تَنْحَصِرُ، منها:

١.   أنْ يَقُولَ ‹الشَّخْصُ› لِمُسْلِمٍ: «يا كافِرُ»، أو «يا يَهُودِيُّ»، أو «يا نَصْرانيُّ»، أو «يا عَدِيمَ الدِّينِ»، مُرِيدًا أنَّ الَّذِي عليه المُخاطَبُ مِنَ الدِّينِ كُفْرٌ أو يَهُودِيَّةٌ أو نَصْرانِيَّةٌ أو لَيْسَ بِدِينٍ؛

٢.   وكَالسُّخْرِيَةِ بِاسْمٍ مِنْ أسْمائِهِ تَعالَى أو وَعْدِهِ أو وَعِيدِهِ، مِمَّن لا يَخْفَى عليه نِسْبَةُ ذلك إليه سُبْحانَهُ؛

٣.   وكَأنْ يَقُولَ ‹الشَّخْصُ›: «لَوْ أمَرَنِي اللهُ بِكَذا لم أفْعَلْهُ»،

٤. أو ‹يَقُولَ الشَّخْصُ›: «لَوْ صارَتِ القِبْلَةُ في جِهَةِ كَذا ما صَلَّيْتُ إليها»،

٥. أو ‹يَقُولَ الشَّخْصُ›: «لَوْ أعْطانِي اللهُ الجَنَّةَ ما دَخَلْتُها»، مُسْتَخِفًّا، أو مُظهِرًا لِلْعِنادِ، في الكُلِّ؛

٦. وكَأنْ يَقُولَ ‹الشَّخْصُ›: «لَوْ آخَذَنِي اللهُ بِتَرْكِ الصَّلاةِ مَعَ ما أنا فيه مِنَ المَرَضِ ظَلَمَنِي»؛

The third category are statements ‹resulting in disbelief›. They are very numerous and innumerable. They include:

1. [An individual] saying to a Muslim: "Hey, disbeliever!" or "Hey, Jew!" or "Hey, Christian!" or "Hey, religion-less!" intending that whatever religion the addressed person follows is disbelief, Judaism, Christianity, or no religion.
2. Mocking one of the names of Allah Most High, His promise, or His threat—by those from whom it is [typically] not hidden that it [the name] is attributed to Him, Glorified is He.
3. Saying, "Even if Allah had ordered that of me, I would not do it."
4. Saying, "Even if the direction of prayer had changed to this direction, I would not pray facing it."
5. Saying, "If Allah gave me Paradise, I would not enter it"—out of disdain or showing pigheadedness in all of them [i.e., the last three].
6. Saying, "If Allah scolded me for not praying given the sickness I have, He would have wronged me."

٧. أو قالَ ‹الشَّخْصُ› لِفِعْلٍ: «حَدَثَ هذا بِغَيْرِ تَقْدِيرِ اللهِ»؛

٨. أو ‹قالَ الشَّخْصُ›: «لَوْ شَهِدَ عِنْدِي الأنْبِياءُ أو المَلائِكَةُ أو جَمِيعُ المُسْلِمِينَ بِكَذا ما قَبِلْتُهُمْ»؛

٩. أو قالَ ‹الشَّخْصُ›: «لا أفعَلُ كَذا وإنْ كانَ سُنَّةً» بِقَصْدِ الاسْتِهْزاءِ؛

١٠. أو ‹قالَ الشَّخْصُ›: «لَوْ كانَ فُلانٌ نَبِيًّا ما آمَنْتُ به»؛

١١. أو أَعْطَاهُ عَالِمٌ فَتْوَى فَقَالَ ‹الشَّخْصُ›: «أَيْشِ هذا الشَّرْعُ» مُرِيدًا الاسْتِخْفَافَ ‹بِحُكْمِ الشَّرْعِ›؛

7. Saying, concerning an action, "That happened without Allah's decree."
8. Saying, "If the prophets, angels, or the entirety of the Muslims testified in front of me to that, I would not accept it."
9. Saying, "I will not do that, even if it is a Sunnah" with the intent of mockery.
10. Saying, "If so-and-so was a prophet, I would not believe in him."
11. If a scholar gave him a fatwa and then ‹the person› said, "What is this religion?!"—intending contempt ‹for religious rulings›.

١٢. أو قالَ ‹الشَّخْصُ›: «لَعْنَةُ اللهِ على كُلِّ عالِمٍ» مُرِيدًا الاسْتِغْرَاقَ الشَّامِلَ ‹لِعُلَمَاءِ الدِّينِ الإسْلامِيِّ أو› لِأَحَدِ الأنْبِيَاءِ،

١٣. أو قالَ ‹الشَّخْصُ›: «أنا بَرِيءٌ مِنَ اللهِ» أو «مِنَ المَلَائِكَةِ» أو «مِنَ النَّبِيِّ» أو «مِنَ القُرْآنِ» أو «مِنَ الشَّرِيعَةِ» أو «مِنَ الإسْلامِ»؛

١٤. أو قالَ ‹الشَّخْصُ› لِحُكْمٍ حُكِمَ بِهِ مِنْ أحْكَامِ الشَّرِيعَةِ: «لَيْسَ هذا الحُكْمُ» أو «لا أعْرِفُ الحُكْمَ» مُسْتَهْزِئًا بِحُكْمِ اللهِ؛

١٥. أو ‹أوْرَدَ الشَّخْصُ› آيةً مستخفًّا أو مستهزئًا بها، ولو مازحًا، كأَنْ قالَ وقَدْ مَلَأَ وِعاءً: ﴿وَكَأْسًا دِهَاقًا﴾، أو أَفْرَغَ شَرَابًا: ﴿فَكَانَتْ سَرَابًا﴾، أو عِنْدَ وَزْنٍ أو كَيْلٍ: ﴿وَإِذَا كَالُوهُمْ أَوْ وَزَنُوهُمْ يُخْسِرُونَ﴾، أو عِنْدَ رُؤْيَةِ جَمْعٍ: ﴿وَحَشَرْنَاهُمْ فَلَمْ نُغَادِرْ مِنْهُمْ أَحَدًا﴾، بِقَصْدِ الاسْتِخْفَافِ أو الاسْتِهْزَاءِ ‹بِهذِهِ الآياتِ› في الكُلِّ؛ وكذا كل موضع استعمل فيه القرآن بذلك القصد؛ فإنْ كانَ بِغَيْرِ ذلك القَصْدِ ‹ونَحْوِهِ› فَلا يَكْفُرُ لكِنْ قالَ الشَّيْخُ أحْمَدُ بْنُ حَجَرٍ رَحِمَهُ اللهُ: «لا تَبْعُدُ حُرْمَتُهُ»؛

12. Saying: "May Allah's curse be upon every scholar!"—intending it to encompass all ‹scholars of the religion of Islam or› one of the prophets.
13. Saying: "I am free of Allah" or "the angels," or "the Prophet," or "the Quran," or "the Sacred Law," or "Islam."
14. Saying about a judgment that is judged according to the rulings of the Sacred Law: "That is not the ruling," or "I do not know the ruling"—out of mocking Allah's ruling.
15. ‹Mentioning a verse out of contempt for it or to mock it—even in jest—, like› saying, after having filled a container: "And a pure cup" (Q78:34); after emptying a drink: "they shall remain a mere semblance" (Q78:20); when weighing or measuring: "But when they measure out to others or weigh out for them, they are deficient" (Q83:3); or when seeing a group: "and We will gather them and leave not any one of them behind" (Q18:47)—with the intent of contempt or mockery ‹of those verses› in them all. And it is the same for every context where the Quran is used with this intent. But if it is done without this intent ‹or its like›, it is not disbelief. However, Shaykh Aḥmad ibn Ḥajar [al-Haythamī] (may Allah grant him His mercy) said, "Its unlawfulness is not far-fetched."

وَكَذا يَكْفُرُ:

١٦. مَنْ شَتَمَ نَبِيًّا أَو مَلَكًا ‹بِفَتْحِ اللَّامِ، أَي واحِدًا مِنَ المَلائِكَةِ›؛

١٧. أَو قالَ ‹الشَّخْصُ›: «أَكُونُ قَوّادًا إِنْ صَلَّيْتُ»، أَو ‹قالَ›: «ما أَصَبْتُ خَيْرًا مُنْذُ صَلَّيْتُ»، أَو ‹قالَ›: «الصَّلاةُ لا تَصْلُحُ لِي»، بِقَصْدِ الاسْتِخْفافِ بِها، أَو الاسْتِهْزاءِ ‹بِها›، أَو اسْتِحْلالِ تَرْكِها، أَو التَّشاؤُمِ بِها؛

١٨. أَو قالَ ‹الشَّخْصُ› لِمُسْلِمٍ: «أَنا عَدُوُّكَ وعَدُوُّ نَبِيِّكَ»،

١٩. أو ‹قالَ› لِشَرِيفٍ: «أنا عَدُوُّكَ وعَدُوُّ جَدِّكَ» مُرِيدًا النَّبِيَّ صَلَّى اللهُ عليه وسَلَّمَ؛

٢٠. أو ‹أنْ› يَقُولَ ‹الشَّخْصُ› شَيْئًا مِنْ نَحْوِ ‹أي من مثل› هذِهِ الألْفاظِ البَشِعَةِ الشَّنِيعَةِ ‹التي تقدمت›؛

Likewise one disbelieves by:

16. Disparaging a prophet or an angel.
17. Saying: "I would be a pimp if I prayed," or "Nothing good has happened to me since I prayed," or "Prayer does not suit me"—with the intent of contempt for them, mocking them, sanctioning their abandonment, or being pessimistic about them.
18. Saying to a Muslim: "I am your enemy and an enemy of your Prophet."
19. [Saying to] a descendant of the Prophet: "I am your enemy and an enemy of your grandfather"—meaning the Prophet (may Allah bless him and grant him peace).
20. Saying something similar to ‹i.e., equivalent to› these hideous and repugnant phrases ‹that has preceded›.

وقَدْ عَدَّ الشَّيْخُ أَحْمَدُ ابْنُ حَجَرٍ والقاضِي عِياضٌ رَحِمَهُما اللهُ في كِتابَيْهِما «الإعْلامُ» و«الشِّفا» شَيْئًا كَثِيرًا ‹مِنَ المُكَفِّراتِ› ، فَيَنْبَغِي الاطِّلاعُ عليه، فَإنَّ مَنْ لم يَعْرِفِ الشَّرَّ يَقَعْ فيه.

Sheikh Aḥmad ibn Ḥajar [al-Haythamī] and Qāḍī ʿIyāḍ (may Allah grant them both His mercy) in their books *Al-Iʿlām bi qawāṭiʿ al-Islām* and *Al-Shifāʾ* enumerated many things ‹that result in disbelief›. One should examine them «i.e., these two books» since whoever does not know evil, falls into it.

A PRINCIPLE FOR KNOWING MANY [TYPES] OF DISBELIEF

‹قَاعِدَةٌ لِمَعْرِفَةِ كَثِيرٍ مِنَ الكُفْرِ›

وَحَاصِلُ ‹أَيْ حُكْمُ› أَكْثَرِ تِلْكَ العِبَاراتِ يَرْجِعُ إلى ‹قَاعِدَةٍ› أَنَّ كُلَّ عَقْدٍ أَو فِعْلٍ أَو قَوْلٍ يَدُلُّ على اسْتِهَانَةٍ أَو اسْتِخْفَافٍ بِاللهِ، أَو كُتُبِهِ، أَو رُسُلِهِ، أَو مَلَائِكَتِهِ، أَو شَعَائِرِهِ أَو مَعَالِمِ دِينِهِ، أَو أَحْكَامِهِ، أَو وَعْدِهِ، أَو وَعِيدِهِ، كُفْرٌ أَو مَعْصِيَةٌ، فَلْيَحْذَرِ الإِنْسَانُ مِنْ ذلك جَهْدَهُ.

‹تنبيه: لا يعذر من يتكلم بالكفر مازحًا أو غاضبًا أو جاهلًا بالحكم، ولا يمنع المزح ولا الغضب ولا الجهل عنه الوقوع في الكفر.›

    The result ‹i.e., the ruling› of most of those expressions returns to ‹the principle› that every belief, action, or statement that indicates mockery of or contempt for Allah, His books, His messengers, His angels, His rites «i.e., the places where religion is practiced», the manifestations «i.e., indicants» of His religion, His rulings, His promises, His threats—is disbelief or disobedience. So a person must take caution from this as much as possible.

    ‹Warning: Whoever utters disbelief out of jest, anger, or ignorance of the ruling is not excused. Jesting, anger, and ignorance do not prevent falling into disbelief.›

SOME OF THE RULINGS RELATED TO APOSTATES

فَصْلٌ ‹في بَعْضِ أحْكامِ المُرْتَدِّ›

يَجِبُ على مَنْ وَقَعَتْ مِنْهُ رِدَّةٌ ‹أي كَفَرَ بَعْدَ أنْ كانَ مُسْلِمًا›: العَوْدُ فَوْرًا إلى الإسْلامِ: بِالنُّطْقِ بِالشَّهادَتَيْنِ، والإقْلاعِ عَمّا وَقَعَتْ به الرِّدَّةُ؛

ويَجِبُ عليه ‹أيْضًا›: النَّدَمُ على ما صَدَرَ منه، والعَزْمُ على أنْ لا يَعُودَ لِمِثْلِهِ، وقَضاءُ ما فاتَهُ مِنْ واجِباتِ الشَّرْعِ في تِلْكَ المُدَّةِ ‹كالصَّلَواتِ المَفْرُوضَةِ›؛

فإنْ لم يَتُبْ ‹أي فإنْ لم يَرْجِعْ عن كُفْرِهِ بِالشَّهادَتَيْنِ› وَجَبَتِ اسْتِتابَتُهُ ‹أي أمْرُهُ بِالرُّجُوعِ إلى الإسْلامِ بِالشَّهادَتَيْنِ›، ولا يُقْبَلُ منه إلّا الإسْلامُ أو القَتْلُ ‹يُنَفِّذُهُ عليه الخَلِيفَةُ بِشُرُوطٍ مَذْكُورَةٍ في المُطَوَّلاتِ›.

Anyone who falls into apostasy ‹i.e., disbelieves after being a Muslim› is required to return to Islam immediately by uttering the two testifications of faith ‹*al-shahādatayn*› and by desisting from whatever caused his apostasy.

He is ‹also› required to regret what came from him; resolve to not repeat the same thing; and make up whatever religious obligations he missed in the interim ‹like obligatory prayers›.

If he does not repent ‹i.e., if he does not recant his disbelief with the two testifications of faith›, he is asked to repent ‹i.e., he is ordered to return to Islam through the two testifications›. Nothing is accepted from him except Islam or execution. ‹The Caliph executes him according to the conditions mentioned in the long books.›

و‹مِمّا يَتَرَتَّبُ على رِدَّةِ الشَّخْصِ أنَّهُ›:

١. ‹تَذْهَبُ بِها حَسَناتُهُ›،
٢. يَبْطُلُ بِها صَوْمُهُ ‹لِلنَّهارِ الَّذي ارْتَدَّ فيه›، و‹يَبْطُلُ بِها› تَيَمُّمُهُ،
٣. و‹يَبْطُلُ بِها› نِكاحُهُ ‹أي زَواجُهُ› قَبْلَ الدُّخُولِ، وكَذا بعدَهُ إنْ لم يَعُدْ إلى الإسْلامِ في العِدَّةِ،

٤. ولا يَصِحُّ عَقْدُ نِكاحِهِ ‹ولَوْ على مُرْتَدَّةٍ مِثْلِهِ›،

٥. وتَحْرُمُ ذَبِيحَتُهُ ‹وتَكُونُ نَجِسَةً›،

٦. ولا يَرِثُ،

‹Among the consequences of the person's apostasy are:›

1. ‹[Apostasy] removes his good deeds.›
2. [Apostasy] invalidates his fast ‹on the day of his apostasy› and his dry ablution.
3. [Apostasy] that takes place before consummation invalidates the marriage. After consummation, it invalidates the marriage if he does not return to Islam during the waiting period [*ʿiddah*].
4. It is not valid for him to contract a new marriage ‹—not even to an apostate like him›.
5. Whatever [an apostate] slaughters is unlawful [to consume] ‹and is filth›.
6. He does not inherit from others.

٧. ولا يُورَثُ،

٨. ولا يُصَلَّى عليه ‹ويَكْفُرُ مَنْ يُصَلِّي عليه وهو عالِمٌ بِحالِهِ›،

٩. ولا يُغَسَّلُ ‹أي لا يَجِبُ›،

١٠. ولا يُكَفَّنُ ‹أي لا يَجِبُ›،

١١. ولا يُدْفَنُ ‹أي لا يَجِبُ›،

١٢. ‹ويَحْرُمُ دَفْنُهُ في مَدافِنِ المُسْلِمِينَ›،

١٣. ومالُهُ ‹بَعْدَ مَوْتِهِ› فَيْءٌ ‹أي لِمَصالِحِ المُسْلِمِينَ›،

١٤. ‹ويُخَلَّدُ بِلا نِهايَةٍ في العَذابِ إنْ ماتَ على رِدَّتِهِ، كَغَيْرِهِ مِمَّنْ يَمُوتُ على غَيْرِ الإسْلامِ›.

[If he dies an apostate:]

7. He does not pass an inheritance to others.
8. He is not prayed upon. ‹Anyone who prays over him while knowing his situation commits disbelief›.
9. He is not washed ‹i.e., it is not obligatory›.
10. He is not shrouded ‹i.e., it is not obligatory›.
11. He is not buried ‹i.e., it is not obligatory›.
12. ‹It is unlawful to bury him where Muslims are buried.›
13. His wealth ‹after his death› is tribute ‹i.e., for Muslim welfare›.
14. ‹He spends eternity in perpetual torture if he dies an apostate, just like others who die as non-Muslims.›

WHAT IS REQUIRED OF RESPONSIBLE INDIVIDUALS

فَصْلٌ ‹فِيما ما يَجِبُ على المُكَلَّفِ›

يَجِبُ على كُلِّ مُكَلَّفٍ أداءُ جَمِيعِ ما أوْجَبَهُ اللهُ عليه،

ويَجِبُ أنْ يُؤَدِّيَهُ على ما أمَرَهُ اللهُ بِهِ، مِنَ الإتْيانِ بِأرْكانِهِ وشُرُوطِهِ، وتَجَنُّبِ مُبْطِلاتِهِ،

ويَجِبُ عليه أمْرُ مَنْ رَآهُ تارِكًا لِشَيْءٍ منها أو يَأْتِي بِها على غيرِ وَجْهِها ‹بأدائِها على وَجْهِها›،

ويَجِبُ عليه قَهْرُهُ على ذلك إنْ قَدِرَ، وإلّا فَيَجِبُ عليه الإنْكارُ بِقَلْبِهِ إنْ عَجَزَ عن القَهْرِ والأمْرِ، وذلك أضْعَفُ الإيمانِ، أي أقَلُّ ما يَلْزَمُ الإنْسانَ عند العَجْزِ؛

ويَجِبُ تَرْكُ جَمِيعِ المُحَرَّماتِ، ونَهْيُ مُرْتَكِبِها ومَنْعُهُ قَهْرًا منها إنْ قَدِرَ عليه، وإلّا وَجَبَ عليه أنْ يُنْكِرَ ذلك بِقَلْبِهِ ومُفارَقَةُ مَوْضِعِ المَعْصِيَةِ؛

والحَرامُ ما تَوَعَّدَ اللهُ مُرْتَكِبَهُ بِالعِقابِ ووَعَدَ تارِكَهُ بِالثَّوابِ ‹وعَكْسُهُ الواجِبُ›.

Every responsible individual is required to perform everything that Allah has made obligatory upon him.

He is required to perform them as Allah has commanded him to perform them, including bringing their essential elements and conditions, and avoiding their invalidators.

He is required to command whomever he sees omitting one of them «i.e., essential elements or conditions» or performing them in an improper manner. ‹[He commands them] to perform them in the proper manner.› He is required to force them to do that if he is able ‹to force them›. Otherwise, he is required to object to it in his heart if he is not able to compel and order—and this is the weakest of faith, i.e., the least an individual is responsible for when unable.

He is required to abandon everything that is unlawful, to forbid whoever commits them and to prevent them from engaging in them by force if able to do so. Otherwise, he is required to object to that in his heart and leave the place of sin.

"Unlawful" [*ḥarām*] is whatever Allah has threatened with punishment to whoever perpetrates it and promised rewards for whoever abandons it.

‹Its opposite is "obligatory" [*wājib*].›

2

PURIFICATION AND PRAYER

بَابُ الطَّهارَةِ والصَّلاةِ

PRAYER TIMES

فَصْلٌ ‹في أوْقاتِ الصَّلَواتِ المَفْرُوضَةِ›

فَمِنَ الواجِبِ خَمْسُ صَلَواتٍ في اليَوْمِ واللَّيْلَةِ:

١. الظُّهْرُ: ووَقْتُها إذا زالَتِ الشَّمْسُ ‹أي مالَتْ عَنْ وَسَطِ السَّماءِ إلى جِهَةِ الغَرْبِ›، إلى مَصِيرِ ظِلِّ كُلِّ شَيْءٍ مِثْلَهُ غَيْرَ ظِلِّ الاسْتِواءِ؛
٢. والعَصْرُ: ووَقْتُها مِنْ بَعْدِ ‹انْتِهاءِ› وَقْتِ الظُّهْرِ إلى مَغِيبِ الشَّمْسِ؛
٣. والمَغْرِبُ: ووَقْتُها مِنْ بَعْدِ مَغِيبِ الشَّمْسِ، إلى مَغِيبِ الشَّفَقِ الأَحْمَرِ؛
٤. والعِشاءُ: ووَقْتُها مِنْ بَعْدِ ‹انْتِهاءِ› وَقْتِ المَغْرِبِ، إلى طُلُوعِ الفَجْرِ الصّادِقِ؛
٥. والصُّبْحُ: ووَقْتُها مِنْ بَعْدِ ‹انْتِهاءِ› وَقْتِ العِشاءِ إلى طُلُوعِ الشَّمْسِ.

Among what is obligatory are five prayers during the day and night.

1. Noon Prayer: Its time is from when the sun passes the zenith ‹i.e., declines from the middle of the sky towards the west› until the shadow of every object is the same [length] as the object minus its shadow when it [i.e., the sun] is at its highest [point in the sky].
2. Afternoon Prayer: Its time is from after the ‹end of› Noon Prayer's time until the sun disappears.

3. Sunset Prayer: Its time is from after the sun disappears until the red glow [along the horizon] disappears.
4. Night Prayer: Its time is from after the ‹end of› Sunset Prayer's time until the rising of true dawn.
5. Morning Prayer: Its time is from after the ‹end of› Night Prayer's time until the sun rises.

فَتَجِبُ هذِهِ الفُرُوضُ في أَوْقاتِها على كُلِّ مُسْلِمٍ، بالِغٍ، عاقِلٍ، طاهِرٍ؛
فَيَحْرُمُ تَقْدِيمُها على وَقْتِها وتَأْخِيرُها عنه بِغَيْرِ عُذْرٍ؛

فَإِنْ طَرَأَ مانِعٌ (كَحَيْضٍ) بَعْدَما مَضَى مِنْ ‹أَوَّلِ› وَقْتِها ما يَسَعُها ‹بِدُونِ طُهْرِها لِمَنْ هو سَلِيمٌ مِنْ نَحْوِ سَلَسٍ›، و‹ما يَسَعُها مَعَ› طُهْرِها لِنَحْوِ ‹مَرِيضِ› سَلَسٍ، لَزِمَهُ قَضاؤُها؛ أو زالَ المانِعُ وقَدْ بَقِيَ مِنَ الوَقْتِ قَدْرُ تَكْبِيرَةٍ لَزِمَتْهُ، وكَذا ‹يَلْزَمُهُ› ما قَبْلَها إِنْ جُمِعَتْ مَعَها، ‹إذا امْتَدَّتِ السَّلامَةُ مِنَ المانِعِ قَدْرًا يَسَعُ الطهارَةَ والصلاةَ›.

These «five» obligations ‹*furūḍ*›, within their times, are required of every Muslim [who is] mature, of sound mind, and pure [i.e., from menstruation and postpartum bleeding].

It is unlawful to perform them before their time or to delay them beyond their time without an excuse.

One is required to make them up if a preventer (like menstruation «postpartum bleeding, insanity, loss of consciousness, intoxication, and apostasy») arises after a period of time has passed from ‹the beginning of› its time long enough to contain its performance ‹without [taking into account the time required for] obtaining purification for it for someone free of incontinence and its like› and ‹long enough to contain it along with› obtaining purification for it for someone with a ‹medical› condition like incontinence.

But if the preventer ceased while enough time remains to say the opening "*Allāhu Akbar*" ("Allah is most great") one is responsible for it, while also ‹being responsible for› the [prayer that is its] predecessor if it is [one that is permissible to] combine [the current prayer] with it ‹when the duration of being free of the preventer is enough to encompass purification and [both] prayer[s]›.[1]

WHAT IS REQUIRED OF GUARDIANS

فَصْلٌ ‹فِيما يَجِبُ على وُلاةِ الأُمُورِ›

يَجِبُ ‹وُجُوبًا كِفائِيًّا› على وَلِيِّ الصَّبِيِّ والصَّبِيَّةِ المُمَيِّزَيْنِ أنْ يَأْمُرَهما بِالصَّلاةِ ويُعَلِّمَهُما أَحْكامَها بَعْدَ سَبْعِ سِنِينَ ‹قَمَرِيَّةٍ›، ويَضْرِبَهُما على تَرْكِها بَعْدَ عَشْرِ سِنِينَ، كَصَوْم أَطاقاهُ،

ويَجِبُ عليه أَيْضًا تَعْلِيمُهُما ‹مِنَ العَقائِدِ والأَحْكامِ› ما ‹يُمْكِنُهُما فَهْمُهُ، وتَعْلِيمُهُما ما› يَجِبُ ‹بَعْدَ البُلُوغِ› عليهما وما يَحْرُمُ ‹كَذلكَ، وكَذا مَشْرُوعِيَّةُ نَحْوِ السِّواكِ›.

ويَجِبُ على وُلاةِ الأمْرِ ‹أيِ الخَلِيفَةِ ومَنْ يَنُوبُ عنه› قَتْلُ تارِكِ الصَّلاةِ ‹ولَوْ فَرْضًا واحِدًا› كَسَلًا ‹بَعْدَ إنْذارِهِ بِشُرُوطِهِ› إنْ لم يَتُبْ ‹أي إنْ لم يُصَلِّ› ، وحُكْمُهُ ‹أَنَّهُ› مُسْلِمٌ.

ويَجِبُ على كُلِّ مُسْلِمٍ أَمْرُ أَهْلِهِ ‹أي زَوْجَتِهِ وأَهْلِ بَيْتِهِ ومَحارِمِهِ› بِها ‹أي الصَّلاةِ›، وقهرُهُمْ ‹على فِعْلِها إنْ قَصَّرُوا›، وتَعْلِيمُهُمْ أَرْكانَها وشُرُوطَها ومُبْطِلاتِها، و‹كذلكَ› كُلُّ مَنْ قَدِرَ عليه مِنْ غَيْرِهِمْ.

It is required ‹being a communal obligation› for the guardian of an immature male or female who has [reached the age of] discernment to command them to pray and to teach them its rulings after seven ‹lunar› years [of age]. After ten years, [he is required] to strike them for forsaking it—like [he must for] fasting that they can endure.

1 For additional clarification, see *The Accessible Conspectus*, 52–53.

He is also required to teach them what ‹beliefs and rulings› they are able to understand, and to teach them what is obligatory for them and unlawful to them ‹after maturity as well—and likewise what has been legislated, like *siwāk*›.

Those in authority ‹i.e., the Caliph and his representative› are required to execute anyone who forsakes prayer ‹even if just a single obligatory prayer› out of laziness ‹after warning him (according to its conditions)› if he does not repent ‹i.e., if he does not pray›. His legal status is that he is a Muslim.

Every Muslim is required to command his family ‹i.e., his wife, his household, and his kin› to perform it ‹i.e., prayer›, to force them ‹to perform it if they neglect it›, and to teach them its essential elements, conditions, and invalidators. And ‹likewise› everyone else «i.e., from among the aforementioned guardians, authorities, husbands, and kin» who is able to do so.

OBLIGATORY ACTS OF ABLUTION

فَصْلٌ ‹في فُرُوضِ الوُضُوءِ›

ومِنْ شُرُوطِ الصَّلاةِ الوُضُوءُ، وفُرُوضُهُ سِتَّةٌ:

الأَوَّلُ: نِيَّةُ الطَّهارَةِ لِلصَّلاةِ بِالقَلْبِ، أو غَيْرُها مِنَ النِّيّاتِ المُجْزِئَةِ، عِنْدَ غَسْلِ الوَجْهِ؛

الثّاني: غَسْلُ الوَجْهِ جَمِيعِهِ، مِنْ مَنابِتِ شَعْرِ رَأْسِهِ إلى الذَّقَنِ، ومِنَ الأُذُنِ إلى الأُذُنِ، شَعَرًا وبَشَرًا، إلّا باطِنَ لِحْيَةِ الرَّجُلِ وعارِضَيْهِ إذا كَثُفْنَ؛

الثّالِثُ: غَسْلُ اليَدَيْنِ مَعَ المِرْفَقَيْنِ وما عليهما ‹كَشَعْرِ الذِّراعِ›؛

الرابِعُ: مَسْحُ الرّأْسِ أو بَعْضِهِ، ولَوْ شَعْرَةً في حَدِّهِ؛

الخامِسُ: غَسْلُ الرِّجلَيْنِ مَعَ الكَعْبَيْنِ، أو مَسْحُ الخُفِّ إذا كَمَلَتْ شُرُوطُهُ؛

السّادِسُ: التَّرْتِيبُ هٰكذا.

Ablution is among the conditions for prayer. Its obligatory acts are six.

The first is the intention, in the heart, of [obtaining] purification for prayer or another sufficient intention, when washing the face.

The second is washing the face in its entirety from the hairline of the head to the chin and from ear to ear. [One must wash] all hair and skin—except the inside of a man's beard and sideburns when they are thick.

The third is washing the arms «including the hands and forearms, and» including the elbows and whatever is upon them ‹like forearm hair›.

The fourth is wiping the head or a part of it—even a single hair within its area.

The fifth is washing the feet [up to and] including the ankles, or wiping the *khuff*, provided the conditions for wiping are met.

The sixth is ordering them [the obligatory actions] this way.

ABLUTION INVALIDATORS

فَصْلٌ ‹في نَواقِضِ الوُضُوءِ›

وَيَنْقُضُ الوُضُوءَ:

١. ما خَرَجَ مِنَ السَّبِيلَيْنِ إلّا المَنِيَّ؛
٢. ومَسُّ قُبُلِ الآدَمِيِّ أو حَلْقَةِ دُبُرِهِ بِبَطْنِ الكَفِّ بِلا حائِلٍ؛
٣. ولَمسُ ‹الذَّكَرِ› بَشَرَةَ ‹الأُنْثَى› الأَجْنَبِيَّةِ ‹ولو زَوْجَةً› مَعَ كِبَرٍ ‹أو العَكْسُ، فَيَنْتَقِضُ وُضُوءُ اللّامِسِ والمَلْمُوسِ إذا اخْتَلَفَ جِنْسُهُما وكانَ كُلٌّ منهما يُشتَهَى ولم يَكُونا مَحْرَمَيْنِ›؛
٤. وزَوالُ العَقْلِ إلّا نَوْمَ قاعِدٍ مُمَكِّنٍ مَقْعَدَتَهُ.

Ablution is invalidated by

1. Anything that exits the two waste passages [i.e., the front and back, thus including the urethra, vagina, and anus]—except for «an individual's own» ejaculate.
2. Touching a human's genitals [including the scrotum] or the anus with the palm of the hand and without a barrier.
3. ‹A male› touching the skin of an unrelated female ‹even his wife› who has neared or passed the stage of adolescence[2] ‹or the opposite [her touching him]. The ablution of the toucher and the touched is invalidated when they are of different sexes, each one of them is old enough to be desired, and they are not kin›.
4. Loss of consciousness—except the sleep of someone [whose buttocks are] firmly seated while sleeping.

WHAT IS REQUIRED CONSEQUENT TO SOMETHING EXITING THE TWO WASTE PASSAGES

فَصْلٌ ‹فِيما يَجِبُ عَقِبَ ما يَخْرُجُ مِنَ السَّبِيلَيْنِ›

يَجِبُ الاسْتِنْجاءُ مِنْ كُلِّ رَطْبٍ خارِجٍ مِنَ السَّبِيلَيْنِ غَيْرَ المَنِيِّ: ‹بِالغَسْلِ› بِالماءِ إلى أنْ يَطْهُرَ المَحَلُّ؛ أو ‹بِأنْ› يَمْسَحَهُ ثَلاثَ مَسَحاتٍ أو أكْثَرَ، إلى أنْ يَنْقَى المَحَلُّ، وإنْ بَقِيَ الأَثَرُ، بِقالِعٍ، طاهِرٍ، جامِدٍ ‹أي غَيْرِ مائعٍ ولا رَطْبٍ ولا مَطْحُونٍ›، غَيْرِ مُحْتَرَمٍ ‹كَالخُبْزِ›، مِنْ غَيْرِ انْتِقالٍ، وقَبْلَ جَفافٍ ‹وإلّا وَجَبَ الماءُ›.

2 Shaykh al-Nawawi al-Jawi (p55) and others clarify that what is meant here is an individual who is legaly mature or has reached a point of development where they typically become attractive to members of the opposite sex who possess healthy dispositions.

Cleansing oneself from everything wet that exits the two waste passages—except sperm—is required.

[Cleansing is performed by] ‹washing with› water until the affected area becomes pure, or [by] wiping the area three or more times until the affected area becomes clean—even if the effect remains—with something that is rough, pure, solid ‹i.e., not liquid, wet, or powdered›, without sanctity «i.e., not revered» ‹like food›, before it «the wet substance that exited» is transferred «from where it remained after exiting» and before it dries. ‹Otherwise, water is obligatory.›

THE OBLIGATORY ACTS OF THE PURIFICATORY BATH AND WHAT NECESSITATES IT

فَصْلٌ ‹فِي مَا يُوجِبُ الغُسْلَ وفروضِهِ›

ومِنْ شُرُوطِ الصَّلاةِ: الطَّهَارَةُ عَنِ الحَدَثِ الأَكْبَرِ، وهو الغُسْلُ ‹ويَتَيَمَّمُ إِنْ عَجَزَ عنه›،

والَّذي يُوجِبُهُ خَمْسَةُ أَشْيَاءَ: خُرُوجُ المَنِيِّ، والجِمَاعُ، والحَيْضُ، والنِّفَاسُ، والوِلادَةُ.

وفُرُوضُ الغُسْلِ اثْنَانِ:

١. نِيَّةُ رَفْعِ الحَدَثِ الأَكْبَرِ أَو نَحْوُها،

٢. وتَعْمِيمُ جَمِيعِ البَدَنِ بَشَرًا ‹وأَظْفَارًا› وشَعَرًا وإِنْ كَثُفَ ‹بِالماءِ›.

Purification from the state of major ritual impurity—which is bathing ‹and dry ablution when unable to bathe›—is among the conditions of prayer.

It is required in case of five things: ejaculation, intercourse, menstruation, postpartum bleeding, and giving birth.

The obligatory acts of bathing are two:

1. Intending to raise the state of major ritual impurity or its like.
2. Covering the entire body (skin, ‹nails,› and hair—even if it is thick) ‹with water›.

THE CONDITIONS FOR PURIFICATION AND THE ESSENTIAL ELEMENTS OF DRY ABLUTION

فَصْلٌ ‹في شُرُوطِ الطَّهارَةِ وأَرْكانِ التَّيَمُّمِ›

شَرْطُ الطَّهارَةِ:

١-٢. الإسْلامُ، والتَّمْيِيزُ،

٣. وعَدَمُ المانِعِ مِنْ وُصُولِ الماءِ إلى المَغْسُولِ،

٤. والسَّيَلانُ،

٥. وأنْ يَكُونَ الماءُ مُطَهِّرًا، بأنْ: لا يُسْلَبَ اسْمَهُ بِمُخالَطَةِ طاهِرٍ يَسْتَغْنِي الماءُ عنه، وأنْ لا يَتَغَيَّرَ بِنَجِسٍ ولو تَغَيُّرًا يَسِيرًا، وإنْ كانَ الماءُ دُونَ القُلَّتَيْنِ زِيدَ ‹شَرْطانِ آخَرانِ لِيَكُونَ مُطَهِّرًا›: بِأنْ لا يُلاقِيَهُ نَجِسٌ غَيْرُ مَعْفُوٍّ عنه، و‹أنْ› لا ‹يَكُونَ› اسْتُعْمِلَ في رَفْعِ حَدَثٍ أو إزالَةِ نَجَسٍ.

The conditions for purification are:

1–2. [The individual] being a Muslim and having discernment.
3. The absence of anything that prevents water from reaching what is being washed.
4. [The water] flowing.
5. The water being purifying by not having lost its name through mixing with a pure substance that water does not need, and by not changing due to filth—even a slight change. When the water is less than *qullatayn* [approximately 216 liters or 57.1 gallons], ‹two conditions for it to be purifying›

are added: (a) it not encountering inexcusable filth, and (b) it not having been used in lifting the state of impurity or in removing filth.

ومَنْ لم يَجِدِ الماءَ أو كانَ يَضرُّهُ الماءُ تَيَمَّمَ، بَعْدَ دُخُولِ الوَقْتِ، وزَوالِ النَّجاسَةِ ‹الَّتي لا يُعفَى عنها›، ومَعْرِفَةِ القِبْلَةِ،

‹ويَكُونُ› بِتُرابٍ ‹أو رَمْلٍ› خالِصٍ طَهُورٍ له غُبارٌ، في الوَجْهِ واليَدَيْنِ، يُرَتِّبُهُما بِضَرْبَتَيْنِ ‹على الأَقَلِّ›، بِنِيَّةِ اسْتِباحَةِ فَرْضِ الصَّلاةِ، ‹وتَكُونُ النِّيَّةُ› مَعَ النَّقْلِ ومَسْحِ أَوَّلِ الوَجْهِ.

Whoever does not find water or if it[s use] would harm him makes dry ablution after the time has entered, [and after] removing ‹inexcusable› filth and knowing the direction of prayer.

«Dry ablution is performed» by [applying] unadulterated soil ‹or sand› that is purifying and contains dirt to the face «including the nose and the entire beard» and hands «up to and including the elbows», in that order, with two strikes ‹at the minimum› while intending to render prayer permissible ‹with the intention concurrent› with transporting «the soil» and wiping the first part of the face.

WHAT IS UNLAWFUL DUE TO MINOR AND OTHER RITUAL IMPURITIES

فَصْلٌ ‹فِيما يَحْرُمُ بِالحَدَثِ الأَصْغَرِ وغَيْرِهِ›

ومَنِ انْتَقَضَ وُضُوؤُهُ حَرُمَ عليه:

١. الصَّلاةُ،
٢. والطَّوافُ،
٣. وحَمْلُ المُصْحَفِ،

٤. ومَسُّهُ ‹أي المُصْحَفِ، ولو بِحائِلٍ›، إلّا الصَّبِيَّ لِلدِّراسَةِ ‹فَيَجُوزُ تَمْكِينُهُ
مِنَ الحَمْلِ والمَسِّ مَعَ حَدَثِهِ›،

It is unlawful for someone whose ablution is invalidated

1. to perform the prayer,
2. to circumambulate the Kaʿbah, and
3. to carry a printed Quran and
4. to touch it ‹even with a barrier›—except a minor for the sake of study ‹in which case it is permissible to allow him to carry it and touch it despite his ritual impurity›.

وعلى الجُنُبِ ‹تَحْرُمُ›:

١-٤. هذه ‹الأَرْبعُ السّابِقَةُ›،

٥. وقِراءَةُ القُرْآنِ ‹بِصَوتٍ›،

٦. ومُكْثُ المَسْجِدِ ‹لا عُبُورُهُ›،

And ‹it is unlawful› for someone with ritual impurity related to sex:

1–4. to do those ‹preceding four things›,
5. to read the Quran ‹with vocalization›, and
6. to remain in a mosque ‹but not to pass through it›.

وعلى الحائِضِ والنُّفَساءِ ‹تَحْرُمُ›:

١-٦. هٰذه ‹السِّتُّ السّابِقَةُ›،

٧. والصَّوْمُ قَبْلَ الانْقِطاعِ،

٨. وتَمْكِينُ الزَّوْجِ مِنَ الاسْتِمْتاعِ بِما بَيْنَ سُرَّتِها ورُكْبَتِها ‹بِالجِماعِ ولو
بِحائِلٍ، واللَّمْسِ بِلا حائِلٍ ولو بِلا شَهْوَةٍ› قَبْلَ الغُسْلِ ‹الشَّرْعِيِّ›.

And ‹it is unlawful› for a woman during menstruation and postpartum bleeding

1–6. to do those ‹preceding six things›,
7. to fast before [menstruation or postpartum bleeding] ceases, and
8. to enable her husband to enjoy what is between her navel and her knees ‹via intercourse (even with a barrier), or touching without a barrier (even without lust)› before ‹the legally defined› washing.

REMOVING FILTH

فَصْلٌ ‹في النَّجاسَةِ وإزالَتِها›

ومِنْ شُرُوطِ الصَّلاةِ الطَّهارَةُ عَنِ النَّجاسَةِ: في البَدَنِ، والثَّوْبِ، والمَكانِ، والمَحْمُولِ له، ‹كَقِنِّينَةٍ أو مِنْدِيلٍ، في يَدِهِ أو جَيْبِهِ›،

فَإِنْ لاقاهُ نَجِسٌ أو لاقَى ثِيابَهُ أو مَحْمُولَهُ بَطَلَتْ صَلاتُهُ، إلّا أنْ يُلْقِيَهُ حالًا، أو يَكُونَ مَعْفُوًّا عَنْهُ كَدَمِ جُرْحِهِ.

Among the conditions of prayer is being purified from filth located on body, clothing, place, and whatever he carries ‹like a bottle or napkin, in his hands or a pocket›.

If filth touches him, his clothing, or whatever he carries, his prayer is invalidated—unless he discards it [the filth or the filthy article] immediately or it is excusable, like blood from his wound.

ويَجِبُ إزالَةُ نَجِسٍ لم يُعْفَ عَنْهُ، ‹وذلك›:

‹في النَّجاسَةِ العَيْنِيَّةِ›: بِإزالَةِ العَيْنِ، مِنْ طَعْمٍ ولَوْنٍ ورِيحٍ ‹وحَجْمٍ›، بِالماءِ المُطَهِّرِ،

و‹في النَّجاسَةِ› الحُكْمِيَّةِ ‹أي الَّتِي لا يُدْرَكُ لَها حَجْمٌ ولا لَوْنٌ ولا طَعْمٌ ولا رِيحٌ›: بِجَرْيِ الماءِ ‹المُطَهِّرِ مَرَّةً› عليها،

و‹في النَّجاسَةِ› الكَلْبِيَّةِ: بِغَسْلِها سَبْعًا ‹بِالماءِ المُطَهِّرِ›، إحْداهُنَّ مَمْزُوجَةٌ ‹أي مُكَدَّرَةٌ› بِالتُّرابِ؛ والمُزِيلَةُ لِلْعَيْنِ وإنْ تَعَدَّدَتْ واحِدَةٌ،

ويُشْتَرَطُ ‹في التَّطْهِيرِ مِنَ النَّجاسَةِ› وُرُودُ الماءِ ‹عليها› إنْ كانَ قَلِيلًا ‹أي دُونَ القُلَّتَيْنِ›.

It is obligatory to remove inexcusable filth.

‹Physical filth› is [removed] by removing the substance—its taste, color, smell ‹and volume›—with purifying water.

Legal ‹filth, i.e., what does not have a perceivable volume, color, taste, and smell› «e.g., a dried drop of urine» [is removed] by flowing ‹purifying› water over it ‹a single time›.

Canine ‹filth› «including filth from dogs, pigs, and their offspring; it applies equally to their body, what they lap with their tongues, their sweat, their blood, and others [i.e., not just what their tongue touches]» is [removed] by washing it seven times ‹with purifying water›—one of the times mixed with ‹ie., turbid from› soil. The attempt that removes the substance—even if it takes several tries—is a single time [i.e., a single washing].

It is a condition ‹for purification from filth› that the water travel ‹over the filth› if the water is a small amount ‹i.e. less than *qullatayn*›.

OTHER CONDITIONS FOR PRAYER

فَصْلٌ ‹في شُرُوطٍ أُخْرَى لِلصَّلاةِ›

ومِنْ شُرُوطِ الصَّلاةِ:

١. اسْتِقْبالُ القِبْلَةِ،

٢. ودُخُولُ الوَقْتِ،

٣. والإِسْلامُ، والتَّمْيِيزُ،

٤. والعِلْمُ بِفَرْضِيَّتِها ‹إذا كانَتْ صَلاةً مَفْرُوضَةً›، وأنْ لا يَعْتَقِدَ فَرْضًا مِنْ فُرُوضِها سُنَّةً،

٥. والسَّتْرُ بِما يَسْتُرُ لَوْنَ البَشَرَةِ لِجَمِيعِ بَدَنِ الحُرَّةِ إلّا الوَجْهَ والكَفَّيْنِ، وسَتْرُ ما بَيْنَ السُّرَّةِ والرُّكْبَةِ لِلذَّكَرِ والأَمَةِ، مِنْ كُلِّ الجَوانِبِ لا الأَسْفَلِ.

The conditions for performing a prayer include:

1. Facing the direction of prayer [the *qiblah*].
2. The time entering.
3. [The individual] being a Muslim and having discernment.
4. [The individual] knowing that it is obligatory ‹when the prayer is obligatory› and not believing «a specific» one of its obligatory actions to be [merely] recommended.
5. [The individual] covering [his nakedness] with something that conceals the color of the skin—from all directions except the bottom. For a free woman, it is covering the entire body except for the face and hands. For a male and for a female slave, it is covering what is between the navel and the knees.

PRAYER INVALIDATORS

فَصْلٌ ‹في مُبْطِلاتِ الصَّلاةِ›

وتَبْطُلُ الصَّلاةُ:

١. بِالكَلامِ ولو بِحَرْفَيْنِ ‹غَيْرِ مُفْهِمَيْنِ› أو بِحَرْفٍ مُفْهِمٍ، إلّا إنْ نَسِيَ وقَلَّ،

٢. وبِالأَفْعالِ الكَثِيرَةِ المُتَوالِيَةِ ‹أو مَعًا›، كَثَلاثِ حَرَكاتٍ، ‹ولو ناسِيًا›،

٣. وبِالحَرَكَةِ المُفْرِطَةِ ‹كَوَثْبَةٍ، ولو ناسِيًا›،

٤. وبِزِيادَةِ رُكْنٍ فِعْلِيٍّ ‹عَمْدًا›،

٥. وبِالحَرَكَةِ الواحِدَةِ لِلَّعِبِ ‹ولو خَفِيفَةً›،

٦. وبِالأَكْلِ والشُّرْبِ، إلّا إنْ نَسِيَ وقَلَّ،

٧. وبِنِيَّةِ قَطْعِ الصَّلاةِ، وبِتَعْلِيقِ قَطْعِها ‹على أَمْرٍ ما›، وبِالتَّرَدُّدِ فيه ‹أي في قَطْعِها›،

٨. وبأَنْ يَمْضِيَ رُكْنٌ مَعَ الشَّكِّ في نِيَّةِ التَّحَرُّمِ، أو يَطُولَ زَمَنُ الشَّكِّ،

٩. ‹وبِتَغْيِيرِ النِّيَّةِ، كَأَنْ قَلَبَ فَرْضًا نَفْلًا وعَكْسُهُ، إلّا لِعُذْرٍ شَرْعِيٍّ›.

A prayer is invalidated by:

1. Speaking—even two phonemes ‹that do not convey a meaning› or a single phoneme ‹that conveys a meaning›—unless one forgot and the amount is small.
2. A large number of consecutive ‹or simultaneous› actions, like three movements ‹even forgetfully›.
3. An excessive movement ‹like jumping—even forgetfully›.
4. Adding an essential movement ‹intentionally›.
5. [Adding] a single action playfully ‹even if it is slight›.
6. Food and drink «reaching an internal cavity even without chewing»—unless one forgot and it was a small amount.
7. Intending to interrupt the prayer, making its interruption conditional ‹upon any matter at all› «even one that is typically impossible but not rationally impossible», and being indecisive about it ‹i.e., interrupting the prayer›.
8. Performing an essential element while doubting that one uttered the initial "*Allāhu akbar,*" «doubting that one uttered it at all, or uttered it completely, or what was intended» or when the doubt «about the intention» is long-lasting.
9. ‹Changing the intention, like converting an obligatory prayer into a recommended prayer or the opposite—except with a legal excuse.›

CONDITIONS FOR PRAYER BEING ACCEPTED

فَصْلٌ ‹في شُرُوطِ قَبُولِ الصَّلاةِ›

وشُرِطَ، مَعَ ما مَرَّ ‹مِنْ شُرُوطِ صِحَّةِ الصَّلاةِ›، لِقَبُولِها عِنْدَ اللهِ سُبْحانَهُ وتَعالى ‹أي نَيْلِ ثَوابِها ودَرَجاتِها›:

١. أنْ يَقْصِدَ بِها وَجْهَ اللهِ وَحْدَهُ ‹أي وِجْهَةَ طاعَةِ اللهِ›،
٢. وأنْ يَكُونَ مَأْكَلُهُ ومَلْبُوسُهُ ومُصَلّاهُ حَلالًا،
٣. وأنْ يُحضِرَ قَلْبَهُ فيها ‹بِأَنْ يَخْشَعَ قَلْبُهُ للهِ ولَوْ لَحْظَةً›، فَلَيْسَ لَهُ مِنْ صَلاتِهِ إلّا ما عَقَلَ ‹أي وَعَى›،
٤. وأنْ لا يُعْجَبَ بِها.

‹ومَعْنَى صِحَّةِ الصَّلاةِ دُونَ قَبُولِها، أنْ تَسْقُطَ عنه المُطالَبَةُ بِها دُونَ أنْ يَنالَ ثَوابَها الخاصَّ.›

And the conditions for the prayer to be accepted with Allah, Glorified is He and Most High, ‹i.e., to obtain its rewards and ranks›—along with what preceded ‹of conditions for the validity of prayer›—are:

1. To intend it for the sake of Allah alone ‹i.e., for worshiping Allah›.
2. His food, clothing, and place of prayer being lawful.
3. Having the presence of heart during it ‹by humbling his heart for Allah—even for an instant› for he gets nothing from his prayer except what he understood ‹i.e., comprehended›.
4. Not being proud of it. «Being proud of it is seeing oneself worthy of rewards and Paradise for having performed it. Instead, one must see that one deserves torture in the Fire for one's good deeds—to say nothing of one's bad ones—due to the terrible etiquette one has with Allah in them.»

‹What is meant by prayer being valid without being accepted is that one is no longer commanded to perform it but one does not obtain its specific reward.›

THE ESSENTIAL ELEMENTS OF PRAYER

فَصْلٌ ‹في أَرْكانِ الصَّلاةِ›

أَرْكانُ الصَّلاةِ سَبْعَةَ عَشَرَ رُكْنًا:

الأَوَّلُ: نِيَّةٌ بِالقَلْبِ ‹لِفِعْلِ الصَّلاةِ›، ويُعَيِّنُ ذاتَ السَّبَبِ والوَقْتِ، ويَنْوِي الفَرْضِيَّةَ في الفَرْضِ، ‹ومِثالُ النِّيَّةِ الكافِيَةِ أَنْ يَنْوِيَ قائِلًا في ذِهْنِهِ: «أُصَلِّي فَرْضَ الظُّهْرِ»›،

The essential elements of prayer are seventeen.

The first: Intending in the heart ‹to perform prayer›: identifying what has a cause «like the Drought Prayer, greeting the mosque, the prayer recommended after making ablution, the Guidance Prayer, and the like» and time «including Noon Prayer, Afternoon Prayer, and the like»; and intending an obligatory prayer as being an obligation «so he intends the prayer to be obligatory to differentiate it from voluntary prayers». ‹An example of a sufficient intention is to intend, saying within his mind: "I am praying the obligatory Noon Prayer."›

‹الثّانِي›: ويَقُولُ ‹بِلِسانِهِ›، بِحَيْثُ يُسْمِعُ نَفْسَهُ كَكُلِّ رُكْنٍ قَوْلِيٍّ: «اللهُ أَكْبَرُ»، ‹مَعَ اسْتِحْضارِ النِّيَّةِ بِقَلْبِهِ›، وهو ثاني أَرْكانِها،

الثّالِثُ: القِيامُ في الفَرْضِ لِلْقادِرِ،

الرّابِعُ: قِراءَةُ الفاتِحَةِ، بِالبَسْمَلَةِ، والتَّشْدِيداتِ، ومُوالاتِها، وتَرْتِيبِها، وإِخْراجِ الحُرُوفِ مِنْ مَخارِجِها، وعَدَمِ اللَّحْنِ ‹أَيْ الخَطَأِ في الحَرَكاتِ› المُخِلِّ بِالمَعْنَى، ويَحْرُمُ اللَّحْنُ الَّذِي لا يُخِلُّ ‹إِذا تَعَمَّدَهُ›، ولا يُبْطِلُ ‹إِذا لم يتعمده›،

[The second:] Saying ‹with his tongue› so that he hears himself—just like all verbal essential elements—"*Allāhu akbar*" ‹with the intention present in his heart›—and that is the second of its essential elements.

The third: Standing in obligatory prayers—for someone who is able.

The fourth: Reciting *Al-Fātiḥah,* with the *Basmalah* and the doubled letters, successively and in order, pronouncing the phonemes from their place of articulation and without mispronunciation ‹i.e., making mistakes in the vowels› that changes the meaning. Mispronunciation that does not change the meaning is unlawful ‹when it is intended›. This mispronunciation does not invalidate [the prayer] ‹when it is not intended›.

الخامِسُ: الرُّكُوعُ بِأَنْ يَنْحَنِيَ بِحَيْثُ تَنالُ راحَتاهُ رُكْبَتَيْهِ،

السّادِسُ: الطُّمَأْنِينَةُ فيه ‹أي في الركوع› بِقَدْرِ ‹زمن القول› «سُبْحانَ اللهِ» ‹وإن لم يقل شيئًا›،

السّابِعُ: الاعْتِدالُ بِأَنْ يَنْتَصِبَ قائِمًا،

الثّامِنُ: الطُّمَأْنِينَةُ فيه ‹أي في الاعتدال بالقدر المذكور›،

التّاسِعُ: السُّجودُ مَرَّتَيْنِ بِأَنْ يَضَعَ جَبْهَتَهُ ‹ولَوْ بَعْضَها› على مُصَلّاهُ مَكْشُوفَةً ومُتَثاقِلًا بِها ومُنَكِّسًا ‹أيْ جاعِلًا أَسْفَلَهُ أَعْلَى مِنْ أَعْلاهُ›، ويَضَعَ شَيْئًا مِنْ رُكْبَتَيْهِ، ومِنْ بُطُونِ كَفَّيْهِ، ومِنْ بُطُونِ أَصابِعِ رِجْلَيْهِ،

The fifth: Bowing, by bending so that one's palms reach one's knees.

The sixth: Reposing therein ‹i.e., while in the bowing position› the amount of ‹i.e., the time of saying› "*Subḥān Allāh*" ("Glory be to Allah") ‹even if one does not say anything›.

The seventh: Rising by standing erect.

The eighth: Reposing therein ‹i.e., while erect for the amount mentioned›.

The ninth: Prostrating twice by placing his exposed forehead ‹even just part of it› on his place of prayer, bearing weight through it, head lowered ‹i.e., making the lower portion of his body higher than the upper part›, and placing [on the place of prayer] some part of his knees and the inner surface of his hands and the bottom surface of his toes.

العاشِرُ: الطُّمَأْنِينَةُ فيه ‹أي في السجود بالقدر المذكور›،
الحادِي عَشَرَ: الجُلُوسُ بين السَّجْدَتَيْنِ،
الثاني عَشَرَ: الطُّمَأْنِينَةُ فيه ‹أي في الجلوس بين السجدتين بالقدر المذكور›،
الثّالِثَ عَشَرَ: الجُلُوسُ، لِلتَّشَهُّدِ الأَخِيرِ وما بَعْدَهُ،
الرّابِعَ عَشَرَ: التَّشَهُّدُ الأَخِيرُ، فَـ‹أَكْمَلُهُ أَنْ› يَقُولَ: «التَّحِيّاتُ المُبارَكاتُ الصَّلَواتُ الطَّيِّباتُ للهِ، السَّلامُ عَلَيْكَ أَيُّها النَّبِيُّ ورَحْمَةُ اللهِ وبَرَكاتُهُ، السَّلامُ عَلَيْنا وعلى عِبادِ اللهِ الصّالِحينَ، أَشْهَدُ أَنْ لا إِلَهَ إِلّا اللهُ وأَشْهَدُ أَنَّ مُحَمَّدًا رَسُولُ اللهِ»،

The tenth: Reposing therein ‹i.e., during prostration for the mentioned amount›.

The eleventh: Sitting between the two prostrations.

The twelfth: Reposing therein ‹i.e., during the sitting between the two prostrations for the mentioned amount›.

The thirteenth: Sitting for the final *tashahhud* and what follows it.

The fourteenth: The final *tashahhud*. ‹For the most complete form› one says:

> "*Al-Taḥiyyātu l-mubārakātu ṣ-ṣalawātu ṭ-ṭayyibātu li-Llāhi, as-salāmu 'alayka ayyuha n-nabiyyu wa raḥmatu Llāhi wa barakātuhu, as-salāmu 'alaynā wa 'alā 'ibdādi Llāhi ṣ-ṣāliḥīn, ashhadu an lā ilāha illa Llāhu, wa ashhadu anna Muḥammada r-rasūl Llāh.*"
>
> ("Greetings, blessing, and the best of prayers to Allah. Peace be upon you, O Prophet, and the mercy of Allah and

His blessings. Peace be upon us and upon the righteous servants of Allah. I testify that there is no deity except Allah, and I testify that Muḥammad is the Messenger of Allah.")

الخامِسَ عَشَرَ: الصَّلاةُ على النَّبِيِّ صَلَّى اللهُ عليه وسَلَّمَ، ‹و›أَقَلُّها: «اللّٰهُمَّ صَلِّ على مُحَمَّدٍ»،

السّادِسَ عَشَرَ: السَّلامُ، ‹و›أَقَلُّهُ: «السَّلامُ عَلَيْكُمْ»،

السّابِعَ عَشَرَ: التَّرْتِيبُ، فَإِنْ تَعَمَّدَ تَرْكَهُ، كَأَنْ سَجَدَ قَبْلَ رُكُوعِهِ بَطَلَتْ، وإِنْ سَها ‹فَتَرَكَ الرُّكُوعَ مثلا› فَلْيَعُدْ إليه ‹فور تذكره› إلّا أنْ يَكُونَ في مِثْلِهِ أو بَعْدَهُ، فَتَتِمُّ بِهِ رَكْعَتُهُ ‹أي يكفيه المثل عن المتروك›، ولَغا ما سَها بِهِ ‹أي ألغي ما بين المتروك والمثل المفعول؛ فيكمل ما بقي من الركعة التي وقع فيها التذكر، ويأتي بالركعات التي كان عليه فعلها بعدها لو لم يتذكّر، ويتدارك ما تقص من صلاته بالإلغاء، فيأتي بركعة›.

The fifteenth: Supplicating upon the Prophet (may Allah bless him and grant him peace), ‹and› its minimum form is: "*Allāhumma ṣalli ʿalā Muḥammad*" ("May Allah bless Muḥammad")

The sixteenth: The closing salutation, ‹and› its minimum form is: "*As-Salāmu ʿalaykum*" ("Peace be upon you")

The seventeenth: The order. If he deliberately omits it—like by prostrating before bowing—it [the prayer] is invalidated. If he forgets ‹and omits the bowing, for example›, he returns to it ‹immediately upon remembering it› unless he is performing its like or [has performed its like as well as] subsequent actions. In that case, he completes his prayer cycle with it ‹i.e., the like suffices him for what was omitted› and the one he forgot is nullified ‹i.e., everything between what was omitted and the performed likeness is nullified, so he completes what remains of the prayer cycle in which he remembered, performs the prayer cycles that he would still need to perform had he not remembered, and makes up whatever is missing from his prayer due to the nullifications. Through this, he performs a prayer cycle›.

CONGREGATIONAL AND FRIDAY PRAYERS

فَصْلٌ ‹في الجَماعَةِ والجُمُعَةِ›

الجَماعَةُ على الذُّكُورِ، الأَحْرارِ، المُقِيمِينَ، البالِغِينَ، ‹العُقَلاءِ›، غَيْرِ المَعْذُورِينَ، فَرْضُ كِفايَةٍ؛

و‹الجَماعَةُ› في الجُمُعَةِ فَرْضُ عَيْنٍ عليهم ‹أي المَذْكُورِينَ›، إذا كانُوا أَرْبَعِينَ، مُكَلَّفِينَ، ‹مُسْتَوْطِنِينَ›، في أَبْنِيَةٍ ‹فَلا تَجِبُ على أَهْلِ الخِيامِ›، و‹تَجِبُ› على مَنْ نَوَى الإقامَةَ عِنْدَهُمْ أَرْبَعَةَ أَيّامٍ صِحاحٍ ‹أي غَيْرَ يَوْمَي الدُّخُولِ والخُرُوجِ›، وعلى مَنْ بَلَغَهُ ‹بالقُوَّةِ لا بِالفِعْلِ› نِداءُ صَيِّتٍ مِنْ طَرَفٍ يَلِيهِ مِنْ بَلَدِها؛

وشَرْطُها ‹أي الجُمُعَةِ›:

١. وَقْتُ الظُّهْرِ،
٢. وخُطْبَتانِ قَبْلَها فيه ‹أي في وقت الظهر› يَسْمَعُهُما الأَرْبَعُونَ ‹بِالفِعْلِ لو أَصْغَوْا ولم يَكُنْ ضَجَّةٌ›،
٣. وأَنْ تُصَلَّى جَماعَةً بِهِمْ،
٤. وأَنْ لا تُقارِنَها ‹في تَكْبِيرَةِ الإحْرامِ› ولا تَسْبِقَها جُمُعَةٌ بِبَلَدِها ‹إلّا إذا شَقَّ الاقْتِصارُ على واحِدَةٍ›؛

[Praying in a] congregation is a communal obligation for males who are free, resident, adult, ‹of sound mind› and who lack an excuse.

For Friday Prayer, it is a personal obligation for them ‹i.e., the aforementioned› when there are forty of them [and they are] responsible, ‹permanently residing› in structures. ‹It is not obligatory for individuals residing in tents.› And ‹it is an obligation› upon whoever intends to stay with them «i.e., the aforementioned [who are required to perform it]» for [at least] four complete days ‹i.e., not including the days of arrival and departure› and upon whoever would be reached ‹potentially—not actually› by a call performed by a strong-voiced person «standing» at the edge adjacent to its land «i.e., where the Friday Prayer is held».

Its conditions ‹i.e., for Friday Prayer› are [as follows]:

1. [Taking place during] the time of Noon Prayer.
2. That there are two sermons before the prayer ‹i.e., during the time of Noon Prayer›, heard by forty ‹who would actually hear it if they were attentive and there is no clamor›.
3. The prayer is prayed as a congregation with those forty.
4. Its performance is not simultaneous to [during the initial "*Allāhu akbar*"] or preceded by a Friday Prayer in that land ‹unless it is difficult to have just one›.

وأَرْكانُ الخُطْبَتَيْنِ:

١. حَمْدُ اللهِ،
٢. والصَّلاةُ على النَّبِيِّ صَلَّى اللهُ عليه وسَلَّمَ،
٣. والوَصِيَّةُ بالتَّقْوَى،

فيهما ‹أي أنَّ هٰذه الثّلاثَةَ المُتَقَدِّمَةَ أَرْكانٌ في كُلٍّ مِنَ الخُطْبَتَيْنِ›؛

٤. وآيَةٌ مُفْهِمَةٌ، في إحْداهُما؛
٥. والدُّعاءُ ‹بأخرويّ› لِلْمُؤْمِنِينَ، في الثّانِيَةِ؛

The essential elements of the two sermons are:

1. Praising Allah [using a form of "*ḥamd*"].
2. Supplicating upon the Prophet (may Allah bless him and grant him peace) [using a form of "*ṣallā*"].
3. Advising [the congregants] to be mindful of Allah.

In them both ‹i.e., the previous three essential elements exist in each of the sermons›. And:

4. [Reciting] a verse that gives a complete meaning in one of the sermons.
5. Supplicating ‹for matters related to the afterlife› for the believers in the second sermon.

وشُرُوطُهُما:

١. الطَّهارَةُ عَنِ الحَدَثَيْنِ،وعَنِ النَّجاسَةِ في البَدَنِ والمَكانِ والمَحْمُولِ،
٢. وسَتْرُ العَوْرَةِ،
٣. والقِيامُ،
٤. والجُلُوسُ ‹قَدْرَ الطُّمَأْنِينَةِ› بَيْنَهُما،
٥. والوِلاءُ بَيْنَهُما،
٦. ‹والوِلاءُ بَيْنَ أَرْكانِهِما›،
٧. و‹الوِلاءُ› بَيْنَهُما وبَيْنَ الصَّلاةِ،
٨. وأنْ يَكُونا ‹أرْكانُهما› بِالعَرَبِيَّةِ.

Their conditions are:

1. Purity from major and minor ritual impurity, and from filth in the body, place, and whatever is carried.
2. Covering one's nakedness.
3. Standing.
4. Sitting ‹long enough to repose› between the two sermons.
5. The two sermons being consecutive.
6. ‹Each sermon's essential elements being consecutive.›
7. The sermons and the prayer being consecutive.
8. Them ‹their essential elements› being in Arabic.

فَصْلٌ ‹في شُرُوطِ الاقْتِداءِ› CONDITIONS FOR FOLLOWING

يَجِبُ على مَنْ صَلَّى مُقْتَدِيًا في جُمُعَةٍ أو غَيْرِها:

١. أنْ لا يَتَقَدَّمَ على إمامِهِ في المَوْقِفِ والإحْرامِ، بَلْ تُبْطِلُ المُقارَنَةُ في الإحْرامِ، وتُكْرَهُ في غَيْرِهِ إلّا التَّأْمِين؛

٢. ويَحْرُمُ تَقَدُّمُهُ بِرُكْنٍ فِعْلِيٍّ، وتَبْطُلُ بِرُكْنَيْنِ، وكَذا ‹يبطل› التَّأَخُّرُ بِهما لِغَيْرِ عُذْرٍ، وبِأَكْثَرَ مِنْ ثَلاثَةِ أَرْكانٍ طَوِيلَةٍ له ‹أي لِعُذْرٍ›،

٣. وأنْ يَعْلَمَ بِانْتِقالاتِ إمامِهِ ‹بِرُؤْيَتِهِ أو سَماعِ صَوْتِهِ أو رُؤْيَةِ بَعْضِ صَفٍّ يَراهُ أو نَحْوِ ذلك›،

٤. وأنْ يَجْتَمِعا في مَسْجِدٍ أو ثَلاثِمِائَةِ ذِراعٍ،

٥. وأنْ لا يَحُولَ بينهما حائِلٌ يَمْنَعُ الاسْتِطْراقَ ‹أي المُرُورَ العادِيَّ، المُباشَرَ في غَيْرِ مَسْجِدٍ، وغَيْرَ المُباشِرِ في مَسْجِدٍ›،

٦. وأنْ يَتَوافَقَ نَظْمُ صَلاتَيْهِما ‹فَلا تَصِحُّ صُبْحٌ خَلْفَ جِنازَةٍ مَثَلًا›،

٧. وأنْ لا يَتَخالَفا في سُنَّةٍ تَفْحُشُ المُخالَفَةُ فيها ‹كَفِعْلِ التَّشَهُّدِ الأَوَّلِ إذا تَرَكَهُ الإمامُ›،

٨. وأنْ يَنْوِيَ الاقْتِداءَ مَعَ التَّحَرُّمِ في الجُمُعَةِ ‹والمُعادَةِ والمجموعة لمطر والمنذورة جماعة›،

٩. و‹أنْ يَنْوِيَ الاقْتِداءَ› قَبْلَ المُتابَعَةِ ‹في فِعْلٍ أو سَلامٍ› وطُولِ الانْتِظارِ ‹لِأَجْلِ هذه المُتابَعَةِ›، في غَيْرِها ‹أي الجُمُعَةِ والمُعادَةِ والمجموعة لمطر والمنذورة جماعة›،

When someone is led in praying Friday Prayer or any other prayer, it is required that:

1. He does not precede his imam in where he stands and in initiating the prayer. Moreover, simultaneity in initiating the prayer invalidates [it]. Elsewhere, simultaneity is offensive—except when saying "*Āmīn.*"
2. It is unlawful for the follower to precede him «i.e., his imam» by one action that is an essential element. Preceding in two essential elements invalidates the prayer. Likewise, lagging by two essential elements without an excuse ‹invalidates›, as does lagging by more than three long essential elements with it ‹i.e., with an excuse›.
3. He is aware of his imam's transitions ‹by seeing him, hearing his voice, seeing part of a line that sees him, or the like›.
4. They are together in a mosque or «within» three-hundred *dhirā*'s [144 meters or 472.44 feet] «approximately. An addition of three *dhirā*'s is harmless».[3]
5. There is no barrier between them «the imam and the follower» that prevents passing between them ‹what is meant by passing is typical direct passing when outside the mosque, indirect passing when inside the mosque›.
6. The overall structure of their two prayers matches. ‹Morning Prayer behind a Funeral Prayer, for example, is not valid.›
7. They do not diverge in a recommended act resulting in a gross divergence ‹like performing the first *tashahhud* if the imam skips it›.
8. He intends being led when initiating the prayer for Friday Prayer ‹and for prayers that are repeated, or combined due to rain, or vowed to perform in congregation›.
9. ‹He intends being led› before following ‹in an action or closing salutation› and before any prolonged waiting ‹for the sake of this following› in other prayers ‹i.e., other than Friday Prayer, repeated prayers, prayers combined due to rain, and prayers one has vowed to pray in congregation›.

---

3 For the sake of simplicity and memory: 145 meters or 475 feet.

ويَجِبُ على الإمامِ: نِيَّةُ الإمامَةِ ‹أو الجماعة› في الجُمُعَةِ والمُعادَةِ ‹والمجموعة لمطر والمنذورة جماعة›، وتُسَنُّ في غَيْرِهِما.

The imam is required to intend leading ‹or congregation› for Friday Prayer and repeated prayers. ‹And for prayers combined due to rain and vowed to pray in congregation.›

The intention is recommended for other prayers.

FUNERALS

فَصْلٌ ‹في الجِنازَةِ›

غَسْلُ المَيِّتِ، وتَكْفِينُهُ، والصَّلاةُ عليه، ودَفْنُهُ، فَرْضُ كِفايَةٍ، إذا كانَ مُسْلِمًا وُلِدَ حَيًّا؛

ووَجَبَ لِذِمِّيٍّ تَكْفِينٌ، ودَفْنٌ؛

و‹وجب› لِسِقْطٍ مَيِّتٍ ‹ظَهَرَ خَلْقُهُ› غَسْلٌ، وكَفْنٌ، ودَفْنٌ؛ ولا يُصَلَّى عليهما ‹أي الذِّمِّيِّ والسِّقْطِ، فَصَلاةُ الجِنازَةِ على الكافِرِ كُفْرٌ، وعلى السِّقْطِ حَرامٌ›؛

ومَنْ ماتَ في قِتالِ الكُفّارِ بِسَبَبِهِ ‹أي القِتالِ› كُفِّنَ في ثِيابِهِ فَإِنْ لم تَكْفِهِ زِيدَ عَلَيْها ودُفِنَ، ولا يُغَسَّلُ ولا يُصَلَّى عليه ‹أي غَسْلُهُ والصَّلاةُ عليه يَحْرُمانِ›.

Washing the deceased, shrouding him, praying over him, and burying him are communal obligations when the [deceased] is a Muslim who was born alive.

Shrouding and burial are obligatory for a non-Muslim resident of the Islamic state.

Washing, shrouding, and burial are obligatory for a miscarried fetus ‹whose human form is apparent›.

They ‹i.e., the non-Muslim resident and miscarried fetus› are not prayed over. ‹Praying the Funeral Prayer for a non-Muslim is disbelief, and for a dead fetus unlawful.›

Whoever died while battling disbelievers as a result ‹i.e., of the battle› is shrouded in his clothes. If they are insufficient, more are added. He [the deceased] is buried, but he is not washed or prayed upon. ‹Washing and praying upon him are unlawful.›

وأَقَلُّ الغَسْلِ: إزالَةُ النَّجاسَةِ، وتَعْمِيمُ جَمِيعِ بَشَرِهِ وشَعَرِهِ وإِنْ كَثُفَ مَرَّةً بِالماءِ المُطَهِّرِ.

وأَقَلُّ الكَفَنِ: ساتِرُ جَمِيعِ البَدَنِ، وثَلاثُ لَفائِفَ لِمَنْ تَرَكَ تَرِكَةً ‹أي مِيراثًا› زائِدَةً عَنْ دَيْنِهِ ولم يُوصِ بِتَرْكِها ‹أي بِتَرْكِ الزِّيادَةِ على الواحِدَةِ›.

The minimum washing is to remove the filth, to cover all of his body and hair—even if thick—one time, and to use purifying water.

The minimum shrouding is to cover the entire body «if someone else is paying for his shroud, such as when it is paid by an individual who is required to support him, the Muslim treasury, an endowment for funerary preparations, or affluent Muslims. The head of a male pilgrim and the face of a female pilgrim are exceptions [from covering the entire body]». Three shrouds are «the minimum» for someone «whether the deceased is male or female» whose estate exceeds his debts and who did not state so in his will ‹i.e., did state forgoing using more than one›.[4]

وأَقَلُّ الصَّلاةِ عليه ‹أي أركانها›:

١. أَنْ يَنْوِيَ ‹بالقلب ذَكَرٌ ولو صَبِيًّا مُمَيِّزًا› فِعْلَ الصَّلاةِ عليه، والفَرْضَ، ويُعَيِّنَ ‹المَيِّتَ ولو بِالإشارَةِ القَلْبِيَّةِ، ويَقُولَ في ذهنه: «أصلّي فرض الجنازة على هذه الميّت»›،

4 In most of his books, Imām al-Nawawī stated that the official position is that the minimum is to cover the individual's nakedness. cf al-Nawawī, *Rawḍat al-ṭālibīn,* 2:110; al-Anṣārī, *Asnā al-maṭālib,* 1:306; *Fatḥ al-Wahhāb* (via al-Jamal's *Futūḥāt al-wahhāb*), 2:158; al-Shirbīnī, *Mughni al-muḥtāj,* 2:15; *Al-Iqnāʿ,* 1:201; al-Dumyāṭī, *I'yanāt al-ṭālibīn,* 2:129.

٢. ‹ويكبر أولًا فـ›يقول: «اللهُ أَكْبَر»، ‹وهذه تكبيرة الدخول في الصلاة التي لا بدّ أن تكون النية المتقدمة ذكرها مصاحبة لها›، ‹أن يصلّيها›

٣. وهو قائمٌ إنْ قَدِرَ،

٤. ثُمَّ يَقْرَأَ الفاتِحَةَ،

٥. ثُمَّ ‹يكبر ثانيًا فـ› يَقُولَ: «اللهُ أَكْبَر»،

٦. ‹ثم يقول›: «اللّٰهُمَّ صَلِّ على مُحَمَّد»،

٧. ثُمَّ ‹يكبر ثالثًا فـ› يَقُولَ: «اللهُ أَكْبَر»،

٨. ‹ثم يقول›: «اللّٰهُمَّ اغْفِرْ لَهُ» أو «‹اللهم› ارْحَمْهُ»،

٩. ثُمَّ ‹يكبر رابعًا فـ› يَقُولَ: «اللهُ أَكْبَر»،

١٠. ‹ثم يقول›: «السَّلامُ عَلَيْكُمْ»،

ولا بُدَّ فيها مِنْ شُرُوطِ الصَّلاةِ، وتَرْكِ المُبْطِلاتِ، ‹وتَقَدُّمِ غُسْلِ المَيِّتِ عيلها›.

The minimum prayer over him ‹i.e., its essential elements› is:

1. ‹A male, even a minor with discernment› intending ‹in his heart› to perform the prayer over him, and [that the prayer is] obligatory and identifying ‹the deceased, even by using a linguistic device to indicate particularity, like "this," and saying in one's mind: "I pray the obligatory Funeral Prayer on this deceased"›.
2. ‹To make the first saying of "*Allāhu akbar.*" One› says, "*Allāhu akbar.*" ‹This is the one for entering the prayer and the aforementioned intention must accompany it.›
3. ‹He prays› standing if he is able.
4. He then reads *Al-Fātiḥah.*
5. Then ‹the second time› he says, "*Allāhu akbar.*"
6. ‹He then says,› "*Allāhumma ṣalli ʿalā Muḥammad.*"
7. Then ‹the third time› he says, "*Allāhu akbar.*"

8. ⟨Then he says⟩, "*Allāhumma ghfir lahu*" ("O Allah, forgive him") or "⟨*Allāhumma*⟩ *rḥamhu*" ("⟨O Allah,⟩ grant him mercy").
9. Then ⟨the fourth time⟩ he says, "*Allāhu akbar.*"
10. ⟨Then he says⟩, "*As-Salāmu ʿalaykum.*"

The conditions for prayer and omitting invalidators are necessary during it. ⟨It is also a condition that it is preceded by washing the deceased.⟩

وَأَقَلُّ الدَّفْنِ: حُفْرَةٌ تَكْتُمُ رَائِحَتَهُ وَتَحْرُسُهُ مِنَ السِّبَاعِ،
وَيُسَنُّ أَنْ يُعَمَّقَ ⟨القَبْرُ⟩ قَدْرَ قَامَةٍ وَبَسْطَةٍ، وَيُوَسَّعَ،
وَيَجِبُ تَوْجِيهُهُ ⟨أَي المَيِّتِ⟩ إِلَى القِبْلَةِ.

The minimum burial is a hole that conceals its [i.e., the interred body's] smell and protects it from predators.

It is recommended to deepen ⟨the grave⟩ the amount of standing and extending the hands, and to widen it.

It is obligatory to face him ⟨i.e., the deceased⟩ towards the direction of prayer.

3

ZAKAT

بَابُ الزَّكاةِ

WHAT ITEMS OBLIGATE ZAKAT

فَصْلٌ :‹فِيما تَجِبُ فيه الزَّكاةُ›

وتَجِبُ الزَّكاةُ في:

١. الإبِلِ ‹ذُكُورًا وإناثًا›، والبَقَرِ ‹حَتَّى الجَوامِيسِ، ذُكُورًا وإناثًا›، والغَنَمِ ‹الضَّأْنِ والمَعْزِ، ذُكُورًا وإناثًا›،

٢. والتَّمْرِ، والزَّبِيبِ،

٣. والزُّرُوعِ ‹أي الحُبُوبِ› المُقْتاتَةِ حالَةَ الاخْتِيارِ ‹الَّتِي تُجَفَّفُ وتُدَّخَرُ›،

٤. والذَّهَبِ، والفِضَّةِ،

٥. والمَعدِنِ ‹أي الذَّهَبِ والفِضَّةِ عِنْدَ اسْتِخْراجِهِما مِنْ مَنْجَمِهِما›،

٦. والرِّكازِ منهما ‹أي ما وُجِدَ مِمّا دُفِنَ قَبْلَ البِعْثَةِ المُحَمَّدِيَّةِ مِنَ الذَّهَبِ والفِضَّةِ›،

٧. وأمْوالِ التِّجارَةِ،

٨. والفِطْرَةِ ‹بَعْدَ رَمَضانَ›.

Zakat is owed for:

1. Camels ‹male and female›, cattle ‹even buffalo—male and female›, and sheep ‹[i.e.,] sheep and goats—male and female›.
2. Dried dates and raisins.

3. Crops ‹i.e., grains› that are voluntarily used as foodstuffs ‹that are dried and stored›.
4. Gold and silver.
5. Gold and silver ore ‹i.e., when extracting them from their mine›.
6. Gold and silver treasure ‹i.e., buried before Muḥammad (may Allah bless him and grant him peace) was sent as a prophet›.
7. Trade assets.
8. [Zakat] al-Fiṭrah ‹after Ramadan›.

LIVESTOCK — فَصْلٌ ‹في زَكاةِ المَواشِي›

وأوَّلُ نِصابِ الإبِلِ خَمْسٌ، والبَقَرِ ثَلاثُونَ، والغَنَمِ أَرْبَعُونَ، فَلا زَكاةَ قَبْلَ ذلك؛ ولا بُدَّ ‹لِوُجُوبِ الزَّكاةِ فيها›:

١. مِنَ الحَوْلِ بَعْدَ ذلك ‹أي أنْ تُمْضِيَ سَنَةً قَمَرِيَّةً في مِلْكِهِ بَعْدَ بُلُوغِها نِصابًا›،

٢. ومِنَ السَّوْمِ في كَلَأٍ مُباحٍ ‹أي أنْ يَرْعاها مالِكُها أو مَأْذُونُهُ في مَرْعًى غَيْرِ مَمْلُوكٍ›،

٣. وألّا تَكُونَ عامِلَةً ‹في الحِراثَةِ ونَحْوِها›.

فَيَجِبُ في كُلِّ خَمْسٍ مِنَ الإبِلِ: شاةٌ ‹مِنَ الغَنَمِ›؛
وفي أَرْبَعِينَ مِنَ الغَنَمِ: شاةٌ جَذَعَـ‹ةُ› ضَأْنٍ، أو ثَنِيَّـ‹ةُ› مَعْزٍ،
وفي ثَلاثِينَ مِنَ البَقَرِ: تَبِيعٌ،
ثُمَّ إنْ زادَتْ ماشِيَتُهُ على ذلك وَجَبَ عليه أنْ يَتَعَلَّمَ ما أَوْجَبَهُ اللهُ تَعالَى عليه فيها.

The minimum amount of camels for which zakat is owed [*niṣāb al-ibl*] is five; for cows, thirty; for sheep, forty. No zakat is owed before this.

It is essential ‹for zakat to be owed on them›:

1. For a year to pass after this ‹i.e., the passing of a lunar year with him owning them after reaching the minimum amount›.
2. Grazing from common grass ‹i.e., its owner, or whomever he gives permission to, grazes them on unowned pasture›.
3. They are not put to work ‹for planting and the like›.

For every five camels, a single sheep «or goat» is owed.

For forty sheep, a one-year-old sheep or a two-year-old goat is owed.

For thirty cattle, a one-year-old calf is owed.

If his livestock exceeds this, he must learn what Allah Most High has made obligatory for him concerning them.

AGRICULTURE

‹فَصْلٌ في زَكاةِ الزُّرُوعِ›

وأمّا التَّمْرُ والزَّبِيبُ والزُّرُوعُ فَأَوَّلُ نِصابِها خَمْسَةُ أَوْسُقٍ، وهي ثَلاثُمِائَةِ صاعٍ بِصاعِهِ عليه الصَّلاةُ والسَّلامُ، ويُضَمُّ زَرْعُ العامِ بَعْضُهُ إلى بَعْضٍ ‹في حِسابِ النِّصابِ›، ولا يُكَمَّلُ جِنْسٌ بِجِنْسٍ ‹فَلا يُكَمَّلُ قَمْحٌ بِشَعِيرٍ مَثَلًا›؛

وتَجِبُ الزَّكاةُ بِبُدُوِّ الصَّلاحِ ‹لِلْأَكْلِ في الرُّطَبِ والعِنَبِ ولَوْ في حَبَّةٍ›، واشْتِدادِ الحَبِّ ‹في الزُّرُوعِ المُقْتاتَةِ ولَوْ في سُنْبُلَةٍ›،

ويَجِبُ فيها العُشْرُ ‹أي عَشَرَةٌ في المِائَةِ› إنْ لم تُسْقَ بِمُؤْنَةٍ ‹أي كُلْفَةٍ›، ونِصْفُهُ ‹أي خَمسَةٌ في المِائَةِ› إنْ سُقِيتْ بِها، وما زادَ على النِّصابِ أَخْرَجَ منه بِقِسْطِهِ،

ولا زَكاةَ فِيما دُونَ النِّصابِ إلّا أنْ يَتَطَوَّعَ.

The first minimum amount for dried dates, raisins, and crops is five *awsuq* [609.84 kilograms or 1,344.5 pounds], which is 300 ṣāʿs [2.03 liters or 4.29 pints] using his [the Prophet's] ṣāʿ (may Allah bless him and grant him peace).

A single year's crops are combined together ‹in calculating the minimum amount›, but one type does not complete another ‹wheat does not complete barley, for example›.

Zakat becomes owed when its fitness ‹for eating—for dates and grapes› become apparent and grains become strong ‹for foodstuffs—even while in its ears›.

The amount owed from it is one-tenth ‹i.e., 10%› if it is irrigated without cost «such as when it is irrigated by rain or flowing water», and half of it ‹i.e., 5%› if it is irrigated with a cost «such as when it is irrigated using water that has been purchased or stolen, or using an animal or human-powered water-wheel, or transporting the water from its source to the field by animal».

Anything in addition to the minimum amount is calculated according to its proportion.

No zakat is owed for anything below the minimum amount—unless one offers it voluntarily.

MONEY

〈فَصْلٌ في زَكاةِ النَّقْدَيْنِ〉

وأمَّا الذَّهَبُ فَنِصابُهُ عِشْرُونَ مِثْقالًا، والفِضَّةُ مِائَتا دِرْهَمٍ،

ويَجِبُ فِيهِما رُبْعُ العُشْرِ ‹أي اثْنانِ ونِصْفٌ في المِائَةِ›،

وما زادَ فَبِحِسابِهِ،

ولا بُدَّ ‹لِوُجُوبِ الزَّكاةِ› فِيهِما مِنَ الحَوْلِ، إلّا ما حَصَلَ مِنْ مَعدِنٍ ورِكازٍ ‹فَلا يُشْتَرَطُ فِيهِما الحَوْلُ لِوُجُوبِ الزَّكاةِ› فيُخْرِجُها ‹عَمّا بَلَغَ مِنهُما نِصابًا› حالًّا،

‹وفي المَعْدِنِ رُبْعُ العُشْرِ أي اثْنانِ ونِصْفٌ في المِائَةِ›، وفي الرِّكازِ الخُمُسُ ‹أي عِشْرُونَ في المِائَةِ›.

The minimum amount for gold is 20 *mithqāls* [85 grams, 2.37 troy ounces, one *dīnār*], and for silver 200 *dirhams* [595 grams or 19.13 troy ounces].

The amount owed for them is one-quarter of one-tenth ‹i.e., 2.5%›.

Anything in addition «to the minimum amount» is calculated according to its proportion.

The passing of a year is essential ‹for zakat to be owed on them›.

But [its passing] is not essential for what is extracted from mines and treasure ‹since the passing of a year is not a condition on them for zakat being owed›. Zakat is taken from them immediately ‹from whichever of them reached the minimum amount›.

‹One-quarter of one-tenth [2.5%] is owed for ore.

One-fifth [20%] is owed for treasure.›

TRADE ‹فَصْلٌ في وزَكاةِ التِّجارَةِ›

وأمّا زَكاةُ التِّجارَةِ فَنِصابُها نِصابُ ما اشْتُرِيَتْ بِهِ مَنَ النَّقْدَيْنِ، ولا يُعْتَبَرُ ‹في الحِسابِ› إلّا ‹المَوْجُودُ مِنْ مالِ التِّجارَةِ› آخِرَ الحَوْلِ، ويَجِبُ فِيها رُبْعُ عُشْرِ القِيمَةِ ‹أي اثْنانِ ونِصْفٌ في المِائَةِ، ذَهَبًا أو فِضَّةً حَسَبَ ما قُوِّمَتْ بِهِ›.

The minimum amount for zakat on trade is the minimum amount for the gold or silver through which it was bought [i.e., that served as its capital]. Nothing is considered ‹during the calculation› except ‹whatever trade assets exist› at the end of the year.

The amount owed for them is one-quarter of one-tenth of their value ‹i.e., 2.5%, gold or silver, calculated according to whichever it was valued through›.

‹فَائِدَةٌ› ومَالُ الخَلِيطَيْنِ والخُلَطَاءِ كَمَالِ المُنْفَرِدِ فِي النِّصَابِ والمُخْرَجِ إذَا كَمَلَتْ شُرُوطُ الخُلْطَةِ.

‹Beneficial Point:› Property that two or more individuals have mixed together is treated similar to an individual's property with respect to the minimum amount and the amount owed—when the conditions for mixed properties are completed.

ZAKAT AL-FIṬR

‹فَصْلٌ فِي زَكَاةِ الفِطْرِ›

وزَكَاةُ الفِطْرِ تَجِبُ بِإِدْرَاكِ جُزْءٍ مِنْ رَمَضَانَ وجُزْءٍ مِنْ شَوَّالٍ عَلى كُلِّ مُسْلِمٍ، عليه وعلى ‹أيْ عَنْ› مَنْ عليه نَفَقَتُهُمْ إذَا كَانُوا مُسْلِمِينَ، عَلى كُلِّ واحِدٍ صَاعٌ مِنْ غَالِبِ قُوتِ البَلَدِ، إذَا فَضَلَتْ عَنْ دَيْنِهِ وكِسْوَتِهِ ومَسْكَنِهِ وقُوتِهِ وقُوتِ مَنْ عليه نَفَقَتُهُمْ يَوْمَ العِيدِ وليلَتَهُ.

‹ويجوز إخراج زكاة الفطر من أوَّل رمضان، ويحرم تأخيرها إلى غروب يوم العيد.›

Zakat al-Fiṭr is required for anyone who is alive during [both] a segment of Ramadan and a segment of Shawwāl. [It is required] from every Muslim, for himself and for ‹i.e., on behalf of› whomever he is required to support who are Muslims.

The amount owed for each individual is one *ṣāʿ* [2.03 liters or 4.29 pints] of the dominant staple food in the land when it is in excess of his debts, clothing, housing, food, and the food of those he is required to support on the day and night of ʿEid.

‹It is permissible to pay Zakat al-Fiṭr from the beginning of Ramadan. It is unlawful to delay its payment until sunset on the Day of ʿEid.›

ZAKAT RECIPIENTS ‹فَصْلٌ في مُسْتَحِقِّي الزَّكاةِ›

وتَجِبُ النِّيَّةُ في جَمِيعِ أَنْواعِ الزَّكاةِ، ‹وتَصِحُّ› بَعْدَ الإفْرازِ ‹وقَبْلَ الدَّفْعِ أو عِنْدَ الإفراز، أو عند الدفع›.

ويَجِبُ صَرْفُها إلى مَنْ وُجِدَ مِنَ الفُقَراءِ، والمَساكِينِ، والعامِلِينَ عليها، والمُؤَلَّفَةِ قُلُوبُهُمْ، وفي الرِّقابِ، والغارِمِينَ، وفي سَبِيلِ اللهِ، وابْنِ السَّبِيلِ،

ولا يَجُوزُ ولا يُجزِئُ صَرْفُها إلى غَيْرِهِمْ؛ ‹ولا يَجُوزُ دَفْعُها إلى كافِرٍ›.

The intention is required in all forms of zakat ‹with it being valid› after setting it [the zakat obligation] aside ‹and before giving it, or when setting it aside, or when giving it›.

It is obligatory to distribute it to whoever is present from the poor, needy, zakat collection workers, those whose hearts are to be reconciled, to free slaves and debtors, those in the cause of Allah, and wayfarers.

It is not permissible and it does not fulfill [the obligation] to distribute it to anyone else.

‹And it is not permissible to give it to disbelievers.›

4

FASTING

بَابُ الصَّوْمِ

فَصْلٌ ‹فِيمَنْ يَجِبُ عليه الصَّوْمُ ومَنْ يَجُوزُ له الفِطْرُ›

WHO IS REQUIRED TO FAST AND WHO IS ALLOWED TO NOT FAST

يَجِبُ صَوْمُ شَهْرِ رَمَضانَ على كُلِّ مُسْلِمٍ مُكَلَّفٍ؛

ولا يَصِحُّ ‹الصَّوْمُ ولا يَجُوزُ› مِنْ حائِضٍ ونُفَساءَ، ويَجِبُ عليهما القَضاءُ؛

Fasting the month of Ramadan is required of every responsible Muslim.

‹Fasting› is not valid ‹and not permissible› for a woman during menses or postpartum bleeding, and they are required to make it up.

ويَجُوزُ الفِطْرُ...

١. لِمُسافِرٍ سَفَرَ قَصْرٍ، وإنْ لم يَشُقَّ عليه الصَّوْمُ، ‹ويَجِبُ عليه القَضاءُ›؛

٢. و‹يَجُوزُ الفِطْرُ› لمرِيضٍ،

٣. و‹يَجُوزُ الفِطْرُ لـ› حامِلٍ،

٤. و‹يَجُوزُ الفِطْرُ لـ› مُرْضِعٍ،

‹لكِنَّ الثَّلاثَةَ الأُخَرَ: فقط إذا› شَقَّ ‹الصَّوْمُ› عليهم مَشَقَّةً لا تُحتَمَلُ، ‹أو خافُوا ذلك على أنفسهم، أوخافت الأَخِيرَتانِ على وَلَدَيْهِما، يَجُوزُ لَهُمْ› الفِطْرُ،

ويَجِبُ عليهم القَضاءُ، ‹ويَجِبُ على الأَخِيرَتَيْنِ فِدْيَةٌ إنْ أَفْطَرَتا خَوْفًا على وَلَدَيْهِما فقَطْ›.

‹ويجوز الفطر لمن كان يلحقه من الصوم مشقة شديدة، لكبر أو مرض لا يرجى شفاؤه، وعليه الفدية عن كلّ يوم يفطره، ولا قضاء عليه›.

Breaking the fast is permissible for:

1. A traveler on a journey that permits shortening prayer, even if fasting is not difficult for him. ‹It is obligatory for him to make it up.›

2–4. Someone who is sick, pregnant, and nursing.

‹But for the last three, it is only when fasting› is difficult enough to be unbearable ‹or they fear this for themselves, or the last two fear this for their child, it is permissible for them› to break the fast and they are required to make it up. ‹An expiation is required for the last two if they broke it out of fear for the child only.›

‹It is permissible for someone to break the fast if fasting causes them extreme difficulty due to age or sickness they are not expected to recover from. An expiation is required from them for every day they break it, but no makeup is required from them.›

OBLIGATORY ACTS OF FASTING AND ITS CONDITIONS

‹فَصْلٌ في فَرائِضِ الصَّوْمِ وشُرُوطِه›

ويَجِبُ التَّبْيِيتُ ‹في صِيامِ الفَرْضِ، بِأَنْ يَنْوِيَ بَيْنَ الغُرُوبِ والفَجْرِ صِيامَ غَدٍ›، والتَّعْيِينُ ‹بِأَنْ يَسْتَحْضِرَ في ذِهْنِهِ أَنَّهُ يَصُومُ عَنْ رَمَضانَ أو نَذْرٍ أو كَفّارَةٍ أو غَيْرِها› في النِّيَّةِ لِكُلِّ يَوْمٍ،

It is required that the intention be made during the night ‹for obligatory fasts—by intending to fast the next day—at some time between sunset and dawn› and by identifying it ‹by bringing to mind that he is fasting for Ramadan, a vow, an expiation, or something else›—each day.

والإمْساكُ عن ‹المفطرات، أي عن›:

١. الجِماعِ ‹الذي يوجب الغسل›،
٢. و‹إنزال المنيّ بـ› الاسْتِمْناءِ ‹أي التَّسَبُّبِ عَمْدًا بِخُرُوجِ مَنِيِّهِ، أو بالمباشرة بِنَحْوِ مَسٍّ ولو بلا بقصد الإنزال›،
٣. والاسْتِقاءَةِ ‹أي التَّسَبُّبِ عَمْدًا في خَرُوجِ شَيْءٍ مِنْ مَعِدَتِهِ إلى فَمِهِ بِنَحْوِ أُصْبُعِهِ›،
٤. وعن الرِّدَّةِ ‹أي الخُرُوجِ مِنَ الإسْلامِ، بِقَوْلِ كُفْرٍ أو فِعْلِ كُفْرٍ أو اعْتِقادِ كُفْرٍ›،
٥. وعَنْ دُخُولِ عَيْنٍ ‹أي ما له حجم ولو صغيرًا› جَوْفًا ‹ولو بدون أكل ولا شرب›، إلّا رِيقَهُ الخالِصَ الطّاهِرَ مِنْ مَعْدِنِهِ ‹أي مَكانِ وُجُودِهِ الأَصْلِيِّ وهو فَمُهُ›.

And [it is required] to refrain from ‹fast breakers, i.e., from›:

1. Intercourse ‹that would require bathing›.
2. ‹Ejaculation via› masturbation ‹i.e., intentionally causing the release of ejaculate, or via contact (like touching) even without intending ejaculation›.
3. Inducing vomiting ‹i.e., intentionally causing something to exit from his stomach to his mouth, such as through using his finger›.
4. Apostasy ‹i.e., exiting Islam, by saying, performing, or believing what is disbelief›.
5. Introducing any substance ‹i.e., whatever has volume—even if small› into a cavity ‹even without eating or drinking› except plain, pure saliva from its source ‹i.e., its origin, which is the mouth›.

و‹يُشْتَرَطُ لِصِحَّةِ الصَّوْمِ›:

١. أنْ لا يُجَنَّ ولو لَحْظَةً،
٢. وأنْ لا يُغْمَى عليه كُلَّ اليَوْمِ ‹مِنَ الفَجْرِ إلى الغُرُوبِ›، ‹فلا يضر نوم اليوم كلّه، ولا إغماء بعضه›.

‹It is a condition for the validity of fasting:›

1. To not be insane—even for a moment.
2. To not be unconscious during the entire day ‹from sunrise until sunset›.

‹Sleeping all day is not harmful to the fast. Neither is being unconscious for part of it.›

UNLAWFUL FASTING ‹فَصْلٌ فِيما يَحْرُمُ صَوْمُهُ›

ولا يَصِحُّ ‹ولا يَجُوزُ› صَوْمُ:

١. العِيدَيْنِ،
٢. وأيّامِ التَّشْرِيقِ،
٣. وكَذا النِّصْفُ الأَخِيرُ مِنْ شَعْبانَ ويَومُ الشَّكِّ، إلّا أنْ يَصِلَهُ ‹أي النِّصْفَ الأخِيرَ مِنْ شَعبانَ، ويَوْمَ الشَّكِّ› بِما قَبْلَهُ، أو ‹يَصُومَهُ› لِقَضاءٍ أو نَذْرٍ أو وِرْدٍ ‹كاعْتِيادِ سُنَّةِ صَوْمِ الاثْنَيْنِ والخَمِيسِ›.

It is not valid ‹nor is it permissible› to fast:

1. The two Eids.
2. The Days of Tashrīq [the three days immediately after Eid al-Aḍḥā].
3. The second half of Shaʿbān and the Day of Doubt—unless one connects it ‹i.e., the second half of Shaʿbān and the Day

of Doubt› with what is before it or ‹fasts it› as a makeup [fast], a vow, or a set habit [*wird*] ‹like habitually fasting Monday and Thursday›.

INTERCOURSE IN THE DAYTIME DURING RAMADAN

‹فَصْلٌ فِيمَنْ أَفْسَدَ صَوْمَ يَوْمٍ مِنْ رَمَضانَ بِجِماعٍ›

ومَنْ أَفْسَدَ صَوْمَ يَوْمٍ مِنْ رَمَضانَ - ولا رُخْصَةَ له في فِطْرِهِ - بِجِماعٍ، فَعَلَيْهِ ‹وعليها إن طاوعته› الإِثْمُ ‹بفطرهما›، والقَضاءُ فَوْرًا ‹أي بَعْدَ يَوْمِ عِيدِ الفِطْرِ›، و‹على الرجل دون المرأة› كَفّارَةُ ظِهارٍ ‹وهي عِتْقُ رَقَبَةٍ، فَإِنْ لم يَسْتَطِعْ فَصِيامُ شَهْرَيْنِ مُتَتابِعَيْنِ، فَإِنْ لم يَسْتَطِعْ فَتَمْلِيكُ سِتِّينَ مِسْكِينًا لِكُلِّ واحِدٍ مِلْءُ الكَفَّيْنِ مِنْ غالِبِ قُوتِ البَلَدِ›.

Someone who spoiled a fasting day of Ramadan—without having a dispensation [*rukhṣah*] for breaking it—through intercourse ‹and anyone who voluntarily complied with him› bears the sin ‹for them both breaking it› and is required to make it up immediately ‹i.e., after the day of Eid al-Fiṭr›.

And he ‹the man, not the woman› is required to make the expiation [which is the same as the one] for likening one's wife to one's kin [*zihār*]. ‹That expiation is to free an «unimpaired, believing [*mu'min*]» slave. If he is unable, he must fast two months consecutively. If he is unable to fast, he must give sixty poor people, giving each one a volume of the dominant staple food in the land equal to the volume of two hands held together for scooping.›

5

HAJJ

بَابُ الحَجِّ

WHO IS OBLIGATED TO PERFORM HAJJ AND UMRAH

فَصْلٌ ‹فِيمَن يَجِبُ عليه الحَجُّ والعُمْرَةُ›

يَجِبُ الحَجُّ والعُمْرَةُ في العُمْرِ مَرَّةً على المُسْلِمِ، الحُرِّ، المُكَلَّفِ، المُسْتَطِيعِ بِما يُوصِلُهُ ويَرُدُّهُ إلى وَطَنِهِ، فاضِلًا عن دَيْنِهِ، ومَسْكَنِهِ وكِسْوَتِهِ اللّائِقَيْنِ بِهِ، ومُؤْنَةِ مَنْ عليه مُؤْنَتُهُ مُدَّةَ ذَهابِهِ وإيابِهِ.

The Hajj and Umrah Pilgrimages are required once in a lifetime for [every] Muslim who is free; responsible; able to travel there and back to his land; and [has funds] in excess of his debts, suitable housing, and clothing, and to cover whomever he is required to support during the period of his travel there and during his return.

ESSENTIAL ELEMENTS OF HAJJ AND UMRAH

‹فَصْلٌ في أَرْكانِ الحَجِّ والعُمْرَةِ›

وأَرْكانُ الحَجِّ:

١. الإِحْرامُ ‹بِأَنْ يَقُولَ بِقَلْبِهِ: «نَوَيْتُ الحَجَّ وَأَحْرَمْتُ بِهِ لِلَّهِ تَعالَى»[1]›،

1 The editor's phrase "دَخَلْتُ في عَمَلِ الحَجِّ" has been replaced with one that is readily found in books of fiqh.

٢. والوُقوفُ بِعَرَفَة،

٣. والطَّوافُ بِالبَيْتِ،

٤. والسَّعْيُ بَيْنَ الصَّفا والمَرْوَةِ،

٥. والحَلْقُ أو التَّقْصِيرُ ‹للرجل، والتقصير فقط للمرأة؛ والتقصير أَقَلُّهُ لِثَلاثِ شَعَراتٍ مِنَ الرَّأْسِ›،

The essential elements for Hajj are:

1. Entering the state of pilgrimage ‹by saying in his heart: "I indend to perform Hajj and enter into it for the sake of Allah Most High"›.
2. Standing on 'Arafah.
3. Circumambulating the House.
4. Traversing between Safā and Marwah.
5. Shaving or trimming ‹for men, and just trimming for women. The minimum for trimming is three hairs from the head›.

وهي ‹أي الأَرْكانُ المَذْكُورَةُ› إلّا الوُقُوفَ أرْكانُ العُمْرَةِ.

ولِهٰذه الأَرْكانِ فُرُوضٌ وشُرُوطٌ لا بُدَّ مِنْ مُراعاتِها.

They ‹i.e., the aforementioned essential elements›—with the exception of standing [on 'Arafah]—are the essential elements of Umrah.

These essential elements have obligatory actions and conditions that must be observed.

WHAT IS UNLAWFUL TO PILGRIMS

‹فَصْلٌ : فِيما يَحْرُمُ على المُحْرِمِ والمُحْرِمَةِ›

وحَرُمَ على مَنْ أَحْرَمَ ‹ بحجّأو عمرة›:

١. طِيبٌ ‹كَعِطْرٍ›،

٢. ودَهْنُ رَأْسٍ ‹بِزَيْتٍ ونَحْوِهِ›، و‹دَهْنُ› لِحْيَةٍ ‹بِزَيْتٍ ونَحْوِهِ›،

٣. وإزالَةُ ظُفْرٍ و‹إزالَةُ› شَعْرٍ،

٤. وجِماعٌ، ومُقَدِّماتُهُ ‹أي الجماع، كَتَقْبِيلٍ بِشَهْوَةٍ›،

٥. وعَقْدُ نِكاحٍ ‹لَهُ ولِغَيْرِهِ، ولا يَنْعَقِدُ›،

٦. واصْطِيادُ صَيْدٍ مَأْكُولٍ بَرِّيٍّ ‹وَحْشِيٍّ›،

٧. و‹يَحْرُمَ› على ‹الـ›رَجُلِ سَتْرُ رَأْسِهِ، و‹يَحْرُمُ على الرَجُلِ› لُبْسُ مُحِيطٍ بِهِ،

٨. و‹يَحْرُمُ› عليها ‹أي المَرْأَةِ› سَتْرُ وَجْهِها، و‹يَحْرُمُ على المَرْأَةِ لُبْسُ› قُفّازٍ.

Someone who has entered into the state of pilgrimage ‹for Hajj or Umrah› is forbidden from:

1. Using perfume ‹like fragrance›.
2. Greasing the hair or beard ‹with oil and the like›.
3. Removing nails or hair.
4. Intercourse and its precursors ‹like kissing lustfully›.
5. Contracting a marriage ‹for himself or someone else—and it is not legally effective›.
6. Hunting ‹wild› edible land prey.
7. Covering the head and wearing clothing that envelops [his body or a complete part of his body] (for men).
8. Covering the face and wearing gloves (for women).

WHAT BECOMES OBLIGATORY DUE TO PERFORMING AN ACT THAT IS UNLAWFUL DURING PILGRIMAGE

‹فَصْلٌ فِيما يَجِبُ بِفِعْلِ مُحَرَّماتِ الإِحْرامِ›

فَمَنْ فعَلَ شَيْئًا مِنْ هٰذه المُحَرَّماتِ فَعَلَيْهِ الإِثْمُ، والكَفّارَةُ ‹أي الفِدْيَةُ، في غَيْرِ عَقْدِ الزَّواجِ›؛ ويَزِيدُ الجِماعُ بِالإفْسادِ ‹للحجّ والعمرة›، ووُجُوبِ القَضاءِ فَوْرًا ‹أي بِلا تَأْخِيرٍ›، وإتْمامِ الفاسِدِ.

Whoever did any of those unlawful things bears the sin and the expiation ‹for acts other than contracting a marriage›.

Intercourse adds «to the above» that it ruins ‹Hajj and Umrah›, the obligation of making them up immediately ‹i.e., without delay›, and having to finish what was spoiled.

OBLIGATORY ACTS OF HAJJ AND UMRAH

‹فَصْلٌ في واجِباتِ الحَجِّ والعُمْرَةِ›

ويَجِبُ ‹في الحَجِّ والعُمْرَةِ›: أَنْ يُحرِمَ مِنَ المِيقاتِ؛

و‹يَجِبُ› في الحَجِّ:

١. مَبِيتُ مُزْدَلِفَةَ ‹لَحظَةً في النِّصْفِ الثّاني مِنْ لَيْلَةِ العِيدِ›،

٢. و‹مَبِيتُ› مِنًى ‹أَكْثَرَ مِنْ نِصْفِ كُلٍّ مِنْ لَيالي التَّشْرِيقِ›،

٣. ورَمْيُ جَمْرَةِ العَقَبَةِ يَوْمَ النَّحْرِ ‹أي العِيدِ›،

٤. ورَمْيُ الجِمَراتِ الثَّلاثِ أيّامَ التَّشْرِيقِ،

٥. وطَوافُ الوَداعِ.

Entering [into Pilgrimage] at the appointed times and locations is required ‹for Hajj and Umrah›.

And for Hajj ‹these are [also] required›:

1. Spending the night at Muzdalifah ‹for a moment during the second half of the night of Eid›.
2. ‹Spending the night at› Minā ‹for more than half the night, each of the nights of Tashrīq›.
3. Throwing pebbles at the *jamrat al-ʿaqaba* on the Day of Naḥr ‹i.e., Eid›.
4. Throwing pebbles at the *jimarāt* pillars on the Days of Tashrīq.
5. The farewell circumambulation.

HUNTING AND FORAGING WITHIN THE SACRED PRECINCTS

‹فَصْلٌ في حُكْمِ صَيْدِ الحَرَمَيْنِ ونَباتِهِما›

ويَحْرُمُ صَيْدُ الحَرَمَيْنِ ‹المَكِّيِّ والمَدَنِيِّ›، و‹قَطْعُ› نَباتِهِما، على مُحْرِمٍ وحَلالٍ ‹أي غيرِ مُحْرِمٍ›، وتَزِيدُ مَكَّةُ ‹المُكَرَّمَةُ› بِوُجُوبِ الفِدْيَةِ.

It is unlawful to hunt prey within the two Sacred Precincts ‹the Meccan and Medinan›, and to ‹cut› their trees—for those making a pilgrimage and those who are free of it ‹i.e., not making pilgrimage›.

In addition, there is an obligatory expiation for [performing these acts in] Mecca.

6

TRANSACTIONS

بَابُ المُعامَلاتِ

فَصْلٌ ‹فِيما يَجِبُ في المُعامَلاتِ والأَنْكِحَةِ›

WHAT IS REQUIRED IN TRANSACTIONS AND MARRIAGE

يَجِبُ على كُلِّ مُسْلِمٍ مُكَلَّفٍ أنْ لا يَدْخُلَ في شَيْءٍ حَتَّى يَعْلَمَ ما أَحَلَّ اللهُ مِنْهُ وما حَرَّمَ؛ لِأَنَّ اللهَ سُبْحانَهُ تَعَبَّدَنا ‹أي كَلَّفَنا› بِأَشْياءَ فَلا بُدَّ مِنْ مُراعاةِ ما تَعَبَّدَنا بِهِ.

Every responsible Muslim is required to refrain from entering into something until he knows what [part] of it Allah has made lawful and unlawful. Allah, Glorified is He, has ordained things for us ‹i.e., made us responsible for them›, and we must observe whatever Allah has ordained for us.

وقَدْ أَحَلَّ اللهُ البَيْعَ وحَرَّمَ الرِّبا، وقَدْ قَيَّدَ الشَّرْعُ هذا البَيْعَ، المُعَرَّفَ بِآلَةِ التَّعْريفِ، بِقُيُودٍ وشُرُوطٍ وأَرْكانٍ لا بُدَّ مِنْ مُراعاتِها، فَعَلَى مَنْ أَرادَ البَيْعَ والشِّراءَ أنْ يَتَعَلَّمَ ذلك، وإلّا أَكَلَ الرِّبا، شاءَ أَمْ أَبَى، وقَدْ قالَ رَسُولُ اللهِ صَلَّى اللهُ عليه وسَلَّمَ: «التّاجِرُ الصَّدُوقُ يُحْشَرُ يَوْمَ القِيامَةِ مَعَ ‹النَّبِيِّينَ و› الصِّدِّيقِينَ والشُّهَداءِ» ‹رَواهُ التِّرْمِذِيُّ وصَحَّحَهُ›، وما ذاكَ إلّا لِأَجْلِ ما يَلْقاهُ مِنْ مُجاهَدَةِ نَفْسِهِ وهَواهُ وقَهْرِهِما على إجْراءِ العُقُودِ على ما أَمَرَ اللهُ ‹أي الطَّرِيقِ الشَّرْعِيِّ›، وإلّا فَلا يَخْفَى ما تَوَعَّدَ اللهُ ‹بِهِ› مَنْ تَعَدَّى الحُدُودَ؛

Allah Most High has permitted sales and prohibited unlawful gain [*ribā*]. The Sacred Law has restricted "sales" (which has been rendered a proper noun through the definite "*al-*" [i.e., the "sale" that Allah has permitted—not everything referred to as sales]) with qualifiers, conditions, and essential elements that must be observed. Anyone who intends to sell and buy must learn them. Otherwise, he will consume unlawful gain whether he wants to or not. The Messenger of Allah (may Allah bless him and grant him peace) said, "The trusty trader is resurrected on Resurrection Day with ‹the prophets and› the truthful ones and the martyrs." ‹Al-Tirmidhī transmitted it and judged it rigorously authenticated.[1]› This is only because of what he faces of struggling against his lower self [*nafs*] and his whims, and compelling the two to conduct contracts according to what Allah Most High has commanded ‹i.e., the lawful way›. Otherwise, one cannot be unaware of that with which Allah has threatened those who transgress limits.

ثُمَّ إنَّ بَقِيَّةَ العُقُودِ، مِنَ الإجارَةِ والقِراضِ والرَّهْنِ والوَكالَةِ والوَدِيعَةِ والعارِيَّةِ والشَّرِكَةِ والمُساقاةِ وغَيْرِها، كَذلك لا بُدَّ مِنْ مُراعاةِ شُرُوطِها وأرْكانِها.

It is the same for all other contracts (including rentals, personal loans, collateral, acting as an agent, deposits for safe-keeping, lending [items], partnerships, sharecropping, and others): their conditions and essential elements must be observed.

وعَقْدُ النِّكاحِ يَحْتاجُ إلى مَزِيدِ احْتِياطٍ وتَثَبُّتٍ حَذَرًا مِمّا يَتَرَتَّبُ على فَقْدِ ذلك.

The marriage contract is even more in need of additional care and checking to take precautions against what results when they [the conditions] are missing.

1 According to the copies of *Sunan al-Tirmidhi* and scholars who quoted it, Imam al-Tirmidhi said that it is "*ḥasan,*" not "*ṣaḥīḥ.*" See Al-Tirmidhi, 1209.

FORBIDDEN SALES
فَصْلٌ ‹في مَنْهِيّاتٍ مِنَ البُيُوعِ›

يَحْرُمُ الرِّبا فِعْلُهُ وأَكْلُهُ وأَخْذُهُ وكِتابَتُهُ وشَهادَتُهُ وحِيلَتُهُ، وهو ‹أَنْواعٌ مِنها›:

١. بَيْعُ أَحَدِ النَّقْدَيْنِ بالآخَرِ نَسِيئَةً ‹أي لِأَجَلٍ›،

٢. أو ‹بَيْعُ أَحَدِ النَّقْدَيْنِ بِالآخَرِ› بِغَيْرِ تَقابُضٍ ‹في مَجْلِسِ العَقْدِ ولَوْ بِغَيْرِ اشْتِراطِ أَجَلٍ›،

٣. أو ‹بَيْعُ أَحَدِ النَّقْدَيْنِ› بِجِنْسِهِ كَذلك ‹أي نَسِيئَةً أو بِغَيْرِ تَقابُضٍ›،

٤. أو ‹بَيْعُ أَحَدِ النَّقْدَيْنِ بِجِنْسِهِ› مُتَفاضِلًا ‹بِالوَزْنِ›،

٥. و‹بَيْعُ› المَطْعُوماتِ بَعْضِها بِبَعْضٍ كَذلك ‹أي نَسِيئَةً أو بِغَيْرِ تَقابُضٍ ولَوْ بِغَيْرِ جِنْسِهِ، ومُتَفاضِلًا إِنْ كانَ بِجِنْسِهِ›؛

Unlawful gain [*ribā*] is unlawful: doing it, consuming it, recording it [i.e., the contract], witnessing it, tricks to accomplish it. It is ‹of several types, some of which are›:

1. Selling gold or silver for the other on credit ‹i.e., for a term›.
2. ‹Selling gold or silver for the other› without exchanging them on the spot ‹where the contract took place—even without stipulating a term›.
3. ‹Selling either gold or silver› for its own type in that same way ‹i.e., on credit or without exchanging on the spot›.
4. ‹Selling either gold or silver for its own type› with a lack of equality ‹in weight›.
5. ‹Selling› foodstuffs for each other in that same way ‹i.e., on credit or without exchanging on the spot—even for a different type; and a lack of equality—if they are of the same type›.

٦. ويَحْرُمُ بَيْعُ ما لم يَقْبِضْهُ؛

٧. و‹يَحْرُمُ بَيْعُ› اللَّحْمِ بِالحَيَوانِ ‹أي بما هو حيٌّ من البهائم›؛

٨. و‹يَحْرُمُ بَيْعُ› الدَّيْنِ بِالدَّيْنِ؛

٩. و‹يَحْرُمُ› بَيْعِ الفُضُوليِّ ‹وهو مَنْ يَبِيعُ ما لَيْسَ لَهُ عليه مِلْكٌ ولا وِلايَةٌ›؛

١٠. و‹يَحْرُمُ بَيْعُ› ما لم يَرَهُ ‹إلّا في بَيْعِ المَوْصُوفِ في الذِّمَّةِ وفي السَّلَمِ›؛

[These] are unlawful:

6. Selling what one has not possessed.
7. ‹Selling› animal flesh for the animal ‹i.e., for a live animal›.
8. ‹Selling› debts for debts.
9. ‹Sales› performed by an unauthorized, self-appointed agent. ‹A self-appointed agent is someone who sells something that he does not own or have authority over.›
10. ‹Selling› what he has not seen ‹except when selling something that has been described with guaranteed attributes and when ordering goods›.

١١. و‹يَحْرُمُ› بَيْعُ غَيْرِ المُكَلَّفِ وعليه ‹أي الشِّراءُ منه والبَيْعُ له›؛

١٢. و‹يَحْرُمُ بَيْعُ› ما لا مَنْفَعَةَ فيه؛

١٣. أو ‹ما› لا قُدْرَةَ على تَسْلِيمِهِ ‹أي يَحْرُمُ بَيْعُهُ›؛

١٤. أو ‹بَيْعٌ› بِلا صِيغَةٍ ‹فَيَحْرُمُ›؛

١٥. و‹يَحْرُمُ› بَيْعُ ما لا يَدْخُلُ تَحْتَ المِلْكِ كَالحُرِّ والأَرْضِ المَواتِ؛

11. Sales performed by an individual who is not responsible ‹i.e., buying from him and selling to him›.
12. ‹Selling› what is useless.
13. [Selling] what cannot be delivered.
14. [Selling] without a verbal contract [i.e., an offer and acceptance].
15. Selling what cannot be owned—like a freeman and unclaimed lands.

١٦. و‹يَحْرُمُ› بَيْعُ المَجْهُولِ؛

١٧. و‹يَحْرُمُ بَيْعُ› النَّجِسِ، كَالكَلْبِ ‹والدَّمِ› وكُلِّ مُسْكِرٍ ‹مائِعٍ›؛

١٨. و‹يَحْرُمُ بَيْعُ› مُحَرَّمٍ ‹أي ما يَحْرُمُ اسْتِعْمالُهُ مُطْلَقًا› كالطُّنْبُورِ ‹والتِّمْثالِ المُجَسَّمِ لِحَيَوانٍ، والصَّلِيبُ ولو مِنْ ذَهَبٍ ولو لِلزِّينَةِ (ويَكْفُرُ مَنْ يَبِيعُهُ لِمَنْ يَعْلَمُ أَنَّهُ يُرِيدُهُ لِلْكُفْرِ)›؛

١٩. ويَحْرُمُ بَيْعُ الشَّيْءِ الحَلالِ الطّاهِرِ على مَنْ تَعْلَمُ أَنَّهُ يُرِيدُ أَنْ يَعْصِيَ بِهِ ‹كَبَيْعِ العِنَبِ لِمَنْ تَعْلَمُ أَنَّهُ يُرِيدُهُ لِيَصْنَعَ منه خَمْرًا لِلشُّرْبِ المُحَرَّمِ›؛

16. Selling what is unknown.
17. ‹Selling› filth, like a dog, ‹blood,› and all ‹liquid› intoxicants.
18. ‹Selling› what is unlawful ‹i.e., what is unconditionally unlawful to use›, like a *ṭunbūr* [a kind of mandolin] ‹and three-dimensional depictions of living animals, crucifixes—even from gold, and even for decoration. Someone who sells them to someone who one knows wants it for disbelief commits disbelief›.
19. Selling something that is pure and lawful to someone one knows intends to use it for disobedience ‹like selling grapes to someone who one knows intends to use them to produce wine that will be unlawfully drunk.›

٢٠. و‹يَحْرُمُ بَيْعُ› الأَشْياءِ المُسْكِرَةِ ‹ولَوْ طاهِرَةً كَالحَشِيشَةِ›؛

٢١. ولا يَصِحُّ بَيْعُ المُكْرَهِ؛

٢٢. ويَحْرُمُ بَيْعُ المَعِيبِ بِلا إِظْهارٍ لِعَيْبِهِ؛

٢٣. ولا تَصِحُّ قِسْمَةُ تَرِكَةِ مَيِّتٍ، ولا بَيْعُ شَيْءٍ منها، ما لم تُوَفَّ دُيُونُهُ ووَصاياهُ، وتُخرَجْ أُجْرَةُ حَجَّةٍ وعُمْرَةٍ إنْ كانا عليه، إلّا أنْ يُباعَ شَيْءٌ ‹مِنَ التَّرِكَةِ› لِقَضاءِ هٰذه الأَشْياءِ، فَالتَّرِكَةُ كَمَرْهُونٍ بِذلك؛

20. ‹Selling› intoxicants ‹even if they are pure, like hashish›.
21. A forced sale is not valid.
22. Selling something defective without showing its defect.

23. It is not valid to divide a deceased person's estate or to sell anything from it while his debts and bequests remain unfulfilled, and the wages for Hajj and Umrah have not been removed (if they are required of him)—except to sell something ‹from his estate› to execute these things. It is as though his estate is held as collateral for this.

٢٤. كـ‹ذلك يَحْرُمُ بَيْعُ› رَقِيقٍ جَنَى ‹كما يحرم التصرّف بالتركة في النقطة السابقة›، ولَوْ بِأَخْذِ دانِقٍ، ‹منها – و›لا يَصِحُّ بَيْعُهُ، حَتَّى يُؤَدَّى ما بِرَقَبَتِهِ، أَوْ يَأْذَنَ الغَرِيمُ في بَيْعِهِ؛

٢٥. ويَحْرُمُ أنْ يُفَتِّرَ رَغْبَةَ المُشْتَرِي أو البائعِ بَعْدَ اسْتِقْرارِ الثَّمَنِ لِيَبِيعَ عليه أو لِيَشْتَرِيَ منه، وبَعْدَ العَقْدِ في مُدَّةِ الخِيارِ أَشَدُّ؛

٢٦. و‹يَحْرُمُ› أنْ يَشْتَرِيَ الطَّعامَ ‹أي القُوتَ كالقَمْحِ› وَقْتَ الغَلاءِ والحاجَةِ لِيَحْبِسَهُ ويَبِيعَهُ بِأَغْلَى؛

٢٧. و‹يَحْرُمُ› أنْ يَزِيدَ في ‹ثَمَنِ› سِلْعَةٍ لِيَغُرَّ غَيْرَهُ؛

٢٨. و‹يَحْرُمُ› أنْ يُفَرِّقَ بَيْنَ الجارِيَةِ ووَلَدِها قَبْلَ التَّمْيِيزِ ‹بِنَحْوِ بَيْعِ أَحَدِهما دُونَ الآخَرِ›؛

٢٩. و‹يَحْرُمُ› أنْ يَغُشَّ ‹في البَيْعِ، كأن يكتم عيبًا يعرفه›؛

٣٠. أو يَخُونَ في الكَيْلِ والوَزْنِ والذَّرْعِ والعَدِّ؛

٣١. أو يَكْذِبَ ‹في البَيْعِ›؛

Like‹wise, these are unlawful›:

24. ‹Selling› a slave who has committed an assault ‹just like it is unlawful to dispose of the estate in the previous point›—even by taking one *dāniq* «one-sixth of a *dirhām*» ‹from the estate›. Selling him «the slave» is not valid until he clears his liabilities or his creditor authorizes its sale «that item».

25. Sapping the buyer's or seller's interest after the price has settled in order to bid against the other or buy it from him. It is even worse after the contract has occurred during the time for choosing [whether to cancel the sale].
26. Buying food ‹i.e., staple foods, like wheat› when prices are high and supply is low in order to hoard it and sell it at a higher price.
27. Increasing ‹the price of› the item to mislead someone else.
28. Separating a female slave from her child before it reaches discernment ‹by something like selling one of them and not the other›.
29. Committing fraud ‹in sales, like concealing a known defect›.
30. Cheating when measuring volume or weight or length or quantity.
31. Lying ‹during the sale›.

٣٢. ويَحْرُمُ أنْ يَبِيعَ القُطْنَ أو غَيْرَهُ مِنَ البَضائِعِ ويُقْرِضَ المُشْتَرِيَ مَعَهُ دَراهِمَ و‹يَشْتَرِطَ عليه أنْ› يَزِيدَ في ثَمَنِ تِلْكَ البِضاعَةِ لِأَجْلِ القَرْضِ؛
٣٣. و‹يَحْرُمُ› أنْ يُقْرِضَ الحائكَ أو غَيْرَهُ مِنَ الأُجَراءِ و‹يَشْتَرِطَ عليه أنْ› يَسْتَخْدِمَهُ بِأَقَلَّ مِنْ أُجْرَةِ المِثْلِ لِأَجْلِ ذلك القَرْضِ، ويُسَمُّونَ ذلك ‹القَرْضَ في هٰذه المُعامَلَةِ والَّتِي قَبْلَها› الرَّبْطَةَ؛
٣٤. و‹يَحْرُمُ› أنْ يُقْرِضَ الحَرّاثِينَ ‹ويَشْتَرِطَ أنَّهُ يصبر› إلى وَقْتِ الحَصادِ ثُمَّ يَبِيعُونَ عليه طَعامَهُمْ بِأَوْضَعَ مِنَ السِّعْرِ قَلِيلًا ‹فيأخذه مقابل قرضه›، ويُسَمُّونَ ذلك المَقْضِيَّ.

These are unlawful:

32. Selling cotton or some other commodity while lending *dirhams* to the buyer and ‹stipulating that he [the seller]› increase the price of the commodities because of the loan.

33. Lending to a weaver or some other employee while ‹stipulating that he› be employed for less than the typical wage because of that loan. This ‹loan in this transaction and the one before it› is named "*rabṭah.*"
34. Lending to a farmer ‹and stipulating that he wait› until the time of harvest and then buying their food for less than the [fair market] price by a little ‹and he takes it in place of his loan›. This is called "*maqḍī.*"

وكَذا جُمْلَةٌ مِنْ مُعامَلاتِ أَهْلِ هٰذا الزَّمانِ – أو أَكْثَرُها – خارِجَةٌ عَنْ قانُونِ الشَّرْعِ.

Similarly, many (or most) of the transactions of the people of this time are outside the code of the Sacred Law.

فَعَلَى مُرِيدِ رِضا رَبِّهِ ‹أيْ نَيْلِ ثَوابِهِ والفَوْزِ بإِكْرامِهِ›، وسَلامَةِ دِينِهِ ودُنْياهُ، أنْ يَتعَلَّمَ ما يَحِلُّ وما يَحْرُمُ، مِنْ عالِمٍ ،وَرِعٍ، ناصِحٍ، شَفِيقٍ على دِينِهِ؛ فَإِنَّ طَلَبَ الحَلالِ فَرِيضَةٌ على كُلِّ مُسْلِمٍ.

Whoever wishes to please his Lord ‹i.e., obtain His reward and achieve His honor› and safeguard his religion and his life must learn what is lawful and what is prohibited from a scholar who is scrupulous, sincere, and compassionate in his religion «i.e., one who strives to remove difficulties from others»—for seeking the lawful is an obligation upon every Muslim.

فَصْلٌ ‹في النَّفَقاتِ الواجِبَةِ وما يُذْكَرُ مَعَها›

OBLIGATORY SUPPORT AND RELATED THINGS

يَجِبُ على المُوسِرِ نَفَقَةُ أُصُولِهِ المُعْسِرِينَ ‹أي الآباءِ والأُمَّهاتِ الفُقَراءِ› وإنْ قَدِرُوا على الكَسْبِ، ونَفَقَةُ فُرُوعِهِ ‹أي أَوْلادِهِ وأَحْفادِهِ› إذا أَعْسَرُوا وعَجَزُوا عَنِ الكَسْبِ لِصِغَرٍ أو زَمانَةٍ،

An individual who is affluent is required to support his poor parents ‹i.e., his male and female progenitors who are destitute›—even if they are able to earn a livelihood—and his own offspring ‹i.e., his children and grand-children› when they are destitute and unable to earn a livelihood due to young age or chronic illness.

ويَجِبُ على الزَّوْجِ نَفَقَةُ الزَّوْجَةِ ومَهْرُها، وعليه لَها مُتْعَةٌ ‹وهي مالٌ يَتَراضَيانِ عليه أو يُقَدِّرُهُ القاضِي إنْ تَنازَعا› إنْ طَلَّقَها ‹بِلا سَبَبٍ منها›،

A husband is required to support his wife and [provide her with her] marriage gift [*mahr*]. He must also give her an amenity payment [*mut'ah*] ‹which is an amount of money given to her that they agree upon or the judge determines if they disagree› if he divorces her ‹for no fault of hers›.

وعلى مالِكِ العَبِيدِ والبَهائِمِ نَفَقَتُهُمْ، وأنْ لا يُكَلِّفَهُمْ مِنَ العَمَلِ ما لا يُطِيقُونَ، ولا يَضْرِبَهُمْ بِغَيْرِ حَقٍّ؛

An owner of a slave or animal is required to support them. He is not to burden them with work they cannot handle. He does not strike them without justification.

ويَجِبُ على الزَّوْجَةِ طاعَةُ الزَّوْجِ في نَفْسِها إلّا ما لا يحِلُّ، وأنْ لا تَصُومَ ‹نَفْلًا› ولا تَخْرُجَ مِنْ بَيْتِهِ إلّا بِإذْنِهِ.

A wife is required to obey her husband regarding her person «regarding sex and enjoyment» except what is not lawful «e.g., sex during menstruation and postpartum bleeding and anal sex», and not to fast ‹voluntarily› «when he is present» and [not to] exit his house except with his permission.

7

PURIFICATION OF THE SELF

بَابُ تَزْكِيَةِ النَّفْسِ

DUTIES OF THE HEART

فَصْلٌ ‹في واجِباتِ القَلْبِ›

مِنَ الواجِباتِ القَلْبِيَّةِ:

١. الإيمانُ باللهِ ‹كما تَقَدَّمَ بَيانُهُ›،

٢. و‹الإيمانُ› بِما جاءَ عَنِ اللهِ ‹كما تَقَدَّمَ بَيانُهُ›،

٣. والإيمانُ بِرَسُولِ اللهِ ‹كما تَقَدَّمَ بَيانُهُ›،

٤. و‹الإيمانُ› بِما جاءَ عَنْ رَسُولِ اللهِ ‹كما تَقَدَّمَ بَيانُهُ›،

٥. والتَّصْدِيقُ ‹وهو مَعْنَى الإيمانِ›،

The heart's acts of obedience include:

1. Belief in Allah ‹as previously clarified›.
2. ‹Belief› in what has come from Allah ‹as previous clarified›.
3. Belief in the Messenger of Allah ‹as previous clarified›.
4. ‹Belief› in what has come from the Messenger of Allah ‹as previous clarified›.
5. Assertion. ‹It is the meaning of belief [*īmān*]›.

٦. واليَقِينُ ‹وهو عَدَمُ الشَّكِّ فِيما يَجِبُ الإيمانُ بِهِ›،

٧. والإِخْلاصُ وهو العَمَلُ ‹بِالطَّاعَةِ› للهِ وَحْدَهُ،

٨. والنَّدَمُ على المَعاصِي ‹لِكَوْنِها مُخالَفَةً لِأَمْرِ الخالِقِ›،

٩. والتَّوَكُّلُ ‹وهو الاعْتِمادُ› على اللهِ ‹في أُمُورِ الرِّزْقِ والسَّلامَةِ مِنَ الضَّرَرِ وغيرِ ذلك، وعَدَمُ الرُّكُونِ إلى الأَسْبابِ›،

١٠. والمُراقَبَةُ للهِ ‹وهي أنْ يُدِيمَ اسْتِحْضارَ أنَّ اللهَ مُطَّلِعٌ عليه يَعْلَمُ بِهِ ويَراهُ ويَسْمَعُهُ، لِيَدُومَ خَوْفُهُ مِنْ مُخالَفَةِ أَمْرِهِ›،

6. Certainty. ‹It is the absence of doubt concerning what one is required to believe.›
7. Sincerity. It is acting ‹in obedience› to Allah alone.
8. Regretting disobedience ‹for it contravening the Creator's command›.
9. Trusting ‹relying› upon Allah ‹in matters related to provisions, safety from harms and other things, and not relying upon means›.
10. Vigilantly observing Allah. ‹It is constantly keeping in mind that Allah monitors him, knows what he is doing, sees him, and hears him—in order to sustain his fear from contravening His command›.

١١. والرِّضا عَنِ اللهِ ‹وهو التَّسْلِيمُ له تَعالَى وتَرْكُ الاعْتِراضِ عليه سُبْحانَهُ›،

١٢. وحُسْنُ الظَّنِّ بِاللهِ ‹بِأَنْ يَتَذَكَّرَ ما عَوَّدَهُ عليه مِنَ الإحْسانِ فَيَرْجُوَ مِثْلَهُ في المُسْتَقْبَلِ›،

١٣. و‹حُسْنُ الظَّنِّ› بِخَلْقِ اللهِ ‹بِأَلّا يَظُنَّ بِهِمْ سُوءًا بِغَيْرِ قَرِينَةٍ كافِيَةٍ شَرْعًا›،

١٤. وتَعْظِيمُ شَعائرِ اللهِ ‹أي كُلِّ ما جُعِلَ عَلَمًا على طاعَةٍ كَالصَّلاةِ، والمُرادُ تَعْظِيمُ كُلِّ ما عَظَّمَهُ الشَّرْعُ›،

١٥. والشُّكْرُ على نِعَمِ اللهِ ‹أي عَدَمُ اسْتِعْمالِها في مَعْصِيَةٍ›،

11. Contentment with Allah. ‹It is surrendering to Him Most High and abandoning challenging Him, Glorified is He›.

12. Thinking the best of Allah. ‹It is by remembering how He has been generous to him in the past, so he hopes for the same in the future.›
13. ‹Thinking the best› about Allah's creation. ‹It is by not assuming evil of them without a legally sufficient corroboration›.
14. Revering the signs of Allah ‹i.e., everything that Allah made an indicator of obedience, such as prayer. What is intended is everything that the Sacred Law reveres›.
15. Gratitude for Allah's blessings ‹i.e., not using them for disobedience›.

١٦. والصَّبْرُ على أداءِ ما أَوْجَبَ اللهُ ‹أي حبس نفسه على ذلك وإلزامُها به›،

١٧. والصَّبْرُ عَمّا حَرَّمَ اللهُ ‹أي على البُعْدِ عَنِ الحَرامِ›،

١٨. و‹الصَّبْرُ› على ما ابْتَلاكَ اللهُ به ‹بِألّا يَدْفَعَكَ بَلاءٌ إلى مَعْصِيَةٍ›،

١٩. والثِّقَةُ بِالرِّزْقِ ‹أي بِأَنَّ ما كُتِبَ لَكَ أنْ تَنْتَفِعَ بِهِ لَنْ يَفُوتَكَ›،

٢٠. واتِّهامُ النَّفْسِ ‹فِيما تَأْمُرُهُ بِهِ خَشْيَةَ أنْ تَكُونَ تُخادِعُ لِلتَّوَصُّلِ إلى مُحَرَّمٍ›،

16. Patience in performing what Allah has made obligatory ‹i.e., holding himself to perform those [obligations] and holding himself responsible for them›.
17. Patience in what Allah has forbidden ‹i.e., in being distant from it›.
18. Patience in what Allah tests you with ‹by not allowing a test to push you to disobedience›.
19. Trusting in provision ‹i.e., that whatever benefit was written for you will not miss you›.
20. Suspecting the *nafs* ‹in what it commands you to do out of fear that it is a trick to bring you to what is unlawful›.

٢١. وعَدَمُ الرِّضا عنها ‹أي عَنِ النَّفْسِ، بِتَذَكُّرِ تَقْصِيرِها›،

٢٢. وبُغْضُ الشَّيْطانِ ‹بِالمَيْلِ إلى مُخالَفَتِهِ›،

٢٣. وبُغْضُ الدُّنْيا ‹بِعَدَمِ الالْتِفاتِ إلى ما يُلهي منها عَنْ طاعَةِ اللهِ›،

٢٤. وبُغْضُ أَهْلِ المَعاصِي ‹بِالمَيْلِ عنهم، والنُّفُورِ مِنْ مَعاصِيهِمْ، ورَفْضِ الاقْتِداءِ بِهِمْ فيها›،

21. Not being content with it ‹i.e., the *nafs*, by remembering its shortcomings›.
22. Hating Satan ‹by being bent on contravening him›.
23. Hating this world ‹by not turning from obedience to Allah to its diversions›.
24. Hating the people of disobedience ‹by turning away from them, fleeing their disobedience, and refusing to follow them in it›.

٢٥. ومَحَبَّةُ اللهِ ‹تَعالَى بِتَوْطِينِ القَلْبِ على عِبادَتِهِ وَحْدَهُ واتِّباعِ أَوامِرِهِ واجْتِنابِ نَواهِيهِ›،

٢٦. و‹مَحَبَّةُ› كَلامِهِ ‹تَعالَى، بِمُراعاةِ تَعْظِيمِ آياتِهِ والتَّسْلِيمِ له والعَمَلِ بِهِ›،

٢٧. و‹مَحَبَّةُ› رَسُولِهِ ‹سيدنا محمد صَلّى اللهُ عليه وسَلَّمَ، بِالإيمانِ به وتَوْقِيرِهِ والمَيْلِ إلى كَمالِ اتِّباعِهِ›،

٢٨. ‹ومَحَبَّةُ سائِرِ أَنْبِيائِهِ تَعالَى، بالإيمانِ بِهِم وتَعْظِيمِهِمْ›،

٢٩. و‹مَحَبَّةُ› الصَّحابَةِ ‹بِاسْتِحْضارِ فَضْلِهِمْ، بِما لَهُمْ مِنْ سابِقَةٍ في الإسْلامِ، وشَرَفِ بِصُحْبَتِهِمْ لِلنَّبِيِّ، ونُصْرَتِهِمْ لَهُ صَلَّى اللهُ عليه وسَلَّمَ، وتَبْلِيغِهِمْ لِلدِّينِ›،

٣٠. و‹محبَّةُ› الآلِ ‹بِمُراعاتِهِمْ إكْرامًا لِلنَّبِيِّ صَلَّى اللهُ عليه وسَلَّمَ، فَهُمْ أَهْلُهُ وذَوُو قَرابَتِهِ›،

٣١. و‹مَحَبَّةُ المُهاجِرِينَ و›الأَنْصارِ ‹الَّذِينَ نَصَرُوا الدِّينَ مِنْ أَهْلِ مَكَّةَ المُكَرَّمَةِ والمَدِينَةِ المُنَوَّرَةِ، ولا سِيَّما السّابِقِينَ الأَوَّلِينَ منهم›،

٣٢. و‹مَحَبَّةُ› الصّالِحِينَ ‹بِتَعْظِيمِهِمْ والمَيْلِ إِلَيْهِمْ وسُلُوكِ طَرِيقِهِمْ›.

25. Loving Allah ‹most High, by holding the heart to worship Him alone and to follow His commands and avoid His prohibitions›.
26. ‹Loving› His speech ‹Most High, by taking care to revere His signs, submitting to His speech, and acting according to it›.
27. ‹Loving› His Messenger ‹our master Muḥammad (may Allah bless him and grant him peace) by believing in him, respecting him, and inclining towards completely following him›.
28. ‹Loving all His (Most High is He) other Prophets by believing in them and revering them.›
29. ‹Loving› the Companions ‹by bringing to mind their superiority due to their precedence in Islam, their honor for accompanying the Prophet, for supporting him (may Allah bless him and grant him peace) and for propagating the religion›.
30. ‹Loving› his household ‹by taking care of them out of respect to the Prophet (may Allah bless him and grant him peace), for they are his family and his relatives›.
31. ‹Loving the Emigrants [*muhājirīn*] and› the Helpers [*anṣār*] ‹who supported the religion, from Mecca and Medina—especially the very first, earliest ones of them›.
32. ‹Loving› the righteous ‹by revering them, inclining towards them, and traveling their path›.

PRECIOUS ADVICE FROM A DIGNIFIED SCHOLAR

‹فَصْلٌ في نَصِيحَةٍ نَفِيسَةٍ مِنْ عالِمٍ جَلِيلٍ›

وقالَ سَيِّدُنا عَبْدُ اللهِ بْنُ عَلَوِيٍّ الحَدّادُ، رَضِيَ اللهُ عنه ونَفَعَنا بِهِ، في كِتابِهِ «النَّصائحِ الدِّينِيَّةِ» ما مَعْناهُ: «وهٰذه أَوْصافٌ يَجِبُ أَنْ يَتَحَلَّى بِها ويَتَّصِفَ بِها كُلُّ مُؤْمِنٍ»اهـ، وهي قَوْلُهُ قَبْلَ هٰذا بَقَلِيلٍ:

«أَنْ يَكُونَ خاشِعًا، مُتَواضِعًا، خائفًا، وَجِلًا، مُشْفِقًا مِنْ خَشْيَةِ اللهِ تَعالَى، زاهِدًا في الدُّنيا، قانِعًا بِاليَسِيرِ منها، مُنْفِقًا لِلْفاضِلِ عَنْ حاجَتِهِ مِمّا في يَدِهِ، ناصِحًا لِعِبادِ اللهِ تَعالَى، مُشْفِقًا عليهم، رَحِيمًا بِهِم، آمِرًا بِالمَعْرُوفِ، ناهِيًا عَنِ المُنْكَرِ،

مُسارِعًا في الخَيْراتِ، مُلازِمًا لِلْعِباداتِ، دالًّا على الخَيْرِ، داعِيًا إلى الهُدَى، ذا سَمْتٍ وتُؤَدَةٍ، ووَقارٍ وسَكِينَةٍ، حَسَنَ الأَخْلاقِ، واسِعَ الصَّدْرِ، لَيِّنَ الجانِبِ، مَخْفُوضَ الجَناحِ لِلْمُؤْمِنِينَ، لا مُتَكَبِّرًا ولا مُتَجَبِّرًا، ولا طامِعًا في النّاسِ، ولا حَرِيصًا على الدُّنْيا، ولا مُؤْثِرًا لَها على الآخِرَةِ، ولا جامِعًا لِلْمالِ، ولا مانِعًا له عَنْ حَقِّهِ،

ولا فَظًّا ولا جافِيًا ولا غَلِيظًا، ولا مُمارِيًا ولا مُجادِلًا ولا مُخاصِمًا، ولا قاسِيًا، ولا سَيِّئَ الأَخْلاقِ، ولا ضَيِّقَ الصَّدْرِ، ولا مُداهِنًا، ولا مُخادِعًا، ولا غاشًّا، ولا مُقَدِّمًا لِلْأَغْنِياءِ على الفُقَراءِ، ولا مُتَرَدِّدًا على السَّلاطِينِ، ولا ساكِتًا عَنِ الإِنْكارِ عليهم مَعَ القُدْرَةِ،

ولا مُحِبًّا لِلْجاهِ والمالِ والوِلاياتِ، بَلْ يَكُونُ كارِهًا لِذلك كُلِّهِ، لا يَدْخُلُ في شَيْءٍ منه، ولا يُلابِسُهُ، إلّا مِنْ حاجَةٍ أو ضَرُورَةٍ»

انْتَهى كَلامُهُ رَضِيَ اللهُ عنه ونَفَعَنا بِهِ.

Our master ʿAbd Allāh bin ʿAlawī al-Ḥaddād (may Allah be pleased with him and may we benefit from him) in his book *Al-Naṣāʾiḥ al-dīniyyah* said (what means): "Every believer must be adorned and characterized with these attributes"—which are [specified by] him saying a little bit before:

> He is humble, modest, and fearful «of Allah's punishment».
>
> [He] dreads «ruinous acts», and is compassionate «about removing difficulties from people» out of fearing Allah.
>
> [He is] abstinent in this world, content with a little bit of it, and spends what is in his possession in excess of his needs.
>
> [He] sincerely advises the servants of Allah Most High, treats them with compassion, and has mercy for them.
>
> [He] commands the right and forbids the wrong.
>
> [He is] swift to good works, constant in acts of worship, guides to good, and invites to guidance.
>
> [He] possesses gravity, deliberation, dignity, calmness, good character, forbearance, and gentleness.
>
> [He is] gentle with believers.
>
> [He is not] arrogant.
>
> [He does not] throw his weight around, or have aspirations for people.
>
> [He does not] covet this world, prioritize it over the afterlife, amass wealth, or hold it [money] back when it should be spent.
>
> [He is not] rude, harsh, ill-mannered, prone to disputes, argumentative, quarrelsome, or hard «hearted».
>
> [He is not] of bad character, [easily] upset, a sycophant, traitorous, or a cheat.
>
> [He does not] place the rich before the poor, frequently visit rulers, or refrain from rebuking them even though he is able to do so.

> [He does not] love prestige, wealth, or position. Indeed, he despises them all and does not enter or engage in any of them unless out of need or necessity.

Thus end his words. (May Allah be pleased with him and may we benefit from him.)

8

DISOBEDIENCE IN DETAIL

بَابُ بَيانِ المَعاصِي

THE HEART

‹فَصْلٌ في مَعاصِي القَلْبِ›

ومِنْ مَعاصِي القَلْبِ:

١. الرِّياءُ بِأَعْمالِ البِرِّ، وهو العَمَلُ لِأَجْلِ ‹نَيْلِ المَنْزِلَةِ والتَّعْظِيمِ عِنْدَ› النّاسِ، ويُحْبِطُ ثَوابَها ‹إذا قارَنَ العَمَلَ›، كَالعُجْبِ بِطاعَةِ اللهِ تَعالَى ‹المَذْكُورِ في النُّقْطَةِ التّالِيَةِ›؛

٢. ‹والعُجْبُ بِالطاعَةِ›، وهو شُهُودُ العِبادَةِ صادِرَةً عَنِ النَّفْسِ، ‹وتَعْظِيمُ نَفْسِهِ مِنْ أَجْلِها، لِكَوْنِهِ› غائِبًا عَنْ ‹تَذَكُّرِ› المِنَّةِ ‹أي أَنَّها فَضْلٌ مِنَ اللهِ›؛

٣. والشَّكُّ في اللهِ ‹وهو كُفْرٌ›؛

٤. والأَمْنُ مِنْ مَكْرِ ‹أي عِقابِ› اللهِ، ‹ومَعْناهُ الاسْتِرْسالُ في المَعاصِي اتِّكالًا على الرَّحْمَةِ›؛

٥. والقُنُوطُ مِنْ رَحْمَةِ اللهِ، ‹وهو الجَزْمُ بِأَنَّهُ لا بُدَّ أَنْ يُعَذِّبَهُ في الآخِرَةِ›؛

The sins of the heart include:

1. Showing off in pious acts. It is acting for the sake of ‹obtaining a position and reverance from› people. It frustrates rewards ‹when it is concurrent with acts›—just like conceit for an act of obeying Allah Most High ‹mentioned in the following point›.

2. ‹Conceit for worshiping.› It is seeing acts of worship as coming from oneself ‹and glorifying oneself for performing them, since he is› remiss in ‹remembering› the grace ‹i.e., they are a favor from Allah›.
3. Doubt in Allah Most High. ‹It is disbelief.›
4. Feeling secure from the machinations ‹i.e., punishments› of Allah. ‹It means impudently acting out disobedience out of relying upon mercy.›
5. Losing hope in Allah's mercy. ‹It is being certain that there is no escaping being tortured in the afterlife.›

٦. والتَّكَبُّرُ على عِبادِ اللهِ، وهو رَدُّ الحَقِّ، واسْتِحْقارُ النّاسِ، ورُؤْيَتُهُ أَنَّهُ خَيْرٌ مِنْ كَثِيرٍ مِنْ خَلْقِ اللهِ تَعالَى ‹مَعَ أَنَّهُ يَجْهَلُ الخاتِمَةَ›؛

٧. والحِقْدُ، وهو إِضْمارُ العَداوَةِ ‹بِالعَزْمِ على الإضْرارِ بِمُسْلِمٍ، وأمّا› إذا عَمِلَ بِمُقْتَضاهُ ولم يَكْرَهْهُ ‹فهو مَعْصِيَةٌ أُخْرَى›؛

٨. والحَسَدُ، وهو كَراهِيَةُ النِّعْمَةِ على المُسْلِمِ واسْتِثْقالُها ‹عليه› إذا لم يَكْرَهْهُ أو عَمِلَ بِمُقْتَضاهُ؛

٩. والمَنُّ بِالصَّدَقَةِ ‹أي أنْ يُعَدِّدَ على الشَّخْصِ إحْسانَهُ إِلَيْهِ بِقَصْدِ الإيذاءِ›، ويُبْطِلُ ثَوابَها؛

١٠. والإِصْرارُ على الذَّنْبِ ‹وهو تَصْمِيمُ القَلْبِ على تَكْرارِهِ›؛

6. Arrogance over the servants of Allah. It is refusing rights, thinking little of people, seeing oneself as better than many of Allah's creatures (most High is He) ‹even though he does not know his final fate›.
7. Spite. It is concealing enmity ‹by resolving to do harm to a Muslim› if he acts upon it without disliking it ‹it is an additional disobedient act›.
8. Envy. It is disliking a blessing given to a Muslim and finding it [the blessing] heavy ‹upon him› when he does not dislike

it or acts according to it «by wishing that it would transfer from that other person to himself, or be removed from the other person».

9. Recounting one's charity ‹i.e., recounting the good deeds one did to another with the intent of hurting them›. It invalidates rewards.
10. Persisting in a sin. ‹It is the heart's planning to repeat it.›

١١. وسُوءُ الظَّنِّ بِاللهِ ‹وقَدْ يَصِلُ إلى الكُفْرِ›؛
١٢. و‹سُوءُ الظَّنِّ› بِعبادِ اللهِ ‹بِلا مُسَوِّغٍ شَرْعِيٍّ›؛
١٣. والتَّكْذِيبُ بِالقَدَرِ ‹وهو كُفْرٌ›؛
١٤. والفَرَحُ بِالمَعْصِيَةِ منه أو مِنْ غَيْرِهِ؛
١٥. والغَدْرُ ‹وهو نَقْضُ العَهْدِ وخِيانَةُ الأَمانَةِ›، ولو بِكافِرٍ؛

11. Thinking badly of Allah. ‹It can reach the level of disbelief.›
12. ‹Thinking badly› of Allah's servants ‹without a legal justification›.
13. Denying fate. ‹It is disbelief.›
14. Taking delight in one's own disobedience or someone else's.
15. Betrayal. ‹It is breaching contracts and violating trusts›—even against a non-Muslim.

١٦. والمَكْرُ ‹أي الخَدِيعَةُ لِلإضْرارِ›؛
١٧. وبُغْضُ الصَّحابَةِ والآلِ والصّالِحِينَ ‹وبُغْضُ جَمِيعِهِمْ كُفْرٌ›،
١٨. والبُخْلُ بِما أَوْجَبَ اللهُ ‹كمنع الزكاة›،
١٩. والشُّحُّ ‹أي الحِرْصُ على أَخْذِ ما في أَيْدِي النّاسِ ولو بِالحَرامِ›،
٢٠. والحِرْصُ ‹أي الطَّمَعَ في حَقِّ غَيْرِكَ›،

٢١. والاسْتِهانَةُ بِما عَظَّمَ اللهُ ‹وهي كُفْرٌ إنْ كانَتْ بِمَعْنَى الاسْتِخْفافِ، ومَعْصِيَةٌ دُونَ الكُفْرِ إنْ كانَتْ بِمَعْنَى ما يُشْعِرُ بِمُجَرَّدِ الإخْلالِ بِواجِبِ التَّعْظِيمِ›،

٢٢. والتَّصْغِيرُ لِما عَظَّمَ اللهُ مِنْ طاعَةٍ أو مَعْصِيَةٍ أو قُرْآنٍ أو عِلْمٍ ‹شَرْعِيٍّ› أو جَنَّةٍ أو نارٍ، ‹وهو كُفْرٌ›.

16. Machinations ‹i.e., deceptions to commit harm›.
17. Hating the Companions, the Household, and the righteous. ‹Hating all of them is disbelief.›
18. Stinginess in what Allah has obligated ‹e.g., refusing to give zakat.›
19. Avarice ‹i.e., coveting to take what is in other people's hands—even through unlawful means›.
20. Coveting ‹i.e., longing for another person's right›.
21. Disdain for anything Allah has revered. ‹It is disbelief if it has the meaning of contempt. It is a sin lesser than disbelief if it has the meaning of something that feels like simply violating the obligation of reverance.›
22. Ridiculing anything Allah revered, including an act of worship, sin, the Quran, ‹religious› knowledge, Paradise, or Fire. ‹It is disbelief.›

THE STOMACH

فَصْلٌ ‹في مَعاصِي البَطْنِ›

ومِنْ مَعاصِي البَطْنِ:

١. أَكْلُ الرِّبا؛
٢. و‹أَكْلُ› المَكْسِ ‹أي الضَّرائِبِ›؛
٣. و‹أَكْلُ› الغَصْبِ؛

٤. و‹أَكْلُ› السَّرِقَةِ؛
٥. و‹أَكْلُ› كُلِّ مَأْخُوذٍ بِمُعَامَلَةٍ حَرَّمَها الشَّرْعُ؛
٦. وشُرْبُ الخَمْرِ، وحَدُّ الشَّارِبِ ‹أَي عُقُوبَتُهُ المُحَدَّدَةُ في الشَّرْعِ› أَرْبَعُونَ جَلْدَةً لِلْحُرِّ، ونِصْفُها لِلرَّقِيقِ، ولِلإِمامِ الزِّيادَةُ تَعْزِيرًا ‹أَي تَأْدِيبًا›؛

The sins of the stomach include:

1. Consuming unlawful gain [*ribā*].
2. ‹Consuming› tolls ‹i.e., taxes›.
3. ‹Consuming› property stolen via force.
4. ‹Consuming› stolen goods.
5. ‹Consuming› everything taken through a transaction the Sacred Law has forbidden.
6. Drinking wine. The prescribed punishment for drinking ‹i.e., its punishment as prescribed by the Sacred Law› is forty lashes for a freeman and half that for a slave. The Imām can, discretionarily, increase the punishment ‹i.e., for disciplining›.

ومنها...
٧. أَكْلُ ‹وشُرْبُ› كُلِّ مُسْكِرٍ؛
٨. و‹أَكْلُ وشُرْبُ› كُلِّ نَجِسٍ؛
٩. و‹أَكْلُ وشُرْبُ› كُلِّ مُسْتَقْذَرٍ؛
١٠. وأَكْلُ مالِ اليَتِيمِ؛
١١. أو ‹أَكْلُ› الأَوْقافِ على خِلافِ شَرْطِ الواقِفِ؛
١٢. و‹أَكْلُ› المَأْخُوذِ بِوَجْهِ الحَياءِ.

They [the sins of the stomach] include:

7. Consuming ‹and drinking› every intoxicant.
8. ‹Consuming and drinking› every impure substance.

9. ‹Consuming and drinking every› disgusting substance.
10. Consuming an orphan's wealth.
11. ‹Consuming› endowments in a manner contrary to the founder's conditions.
12. ‹Consuming› something acquired through fear of blame. «Whenever he acquires something while knowing that the giver was propelled by fear of blame from him or someone present, and the giver would not have given it to him if not for that—it is unlawful and he must return it.»

THE EYES

‹فَصْلٌ في مَعاصِي العَيْنِ›

وِمِنْ مَعاصِي العَيْنِ:

النَّظَرُ ‹مِنَ الرِّجالِ› إلى النِّساءِ الأَجْنَبِيّاتِ ‹بِشَهْوَةٍ مُطْلَقًا، وبِغيرِ شَهْوَةٍ إذا كانَ إلى غَيْرِ الوَجْهِ والكَفَّيْنِ، وقِيلَ وبِغَيْرِ شَهْوَةٍ إلَيْهِما إذا كانَ لِغَيْرِ حاجَةٍ كَمُعامَلَةٍ›،

وكَذا ‹يَحْرُمُ› نَظَرُهُنَّ إلَيْهِمْ ‹أي نَظَرُ النِّساءِ إلى الرِّجالِ الأجانِبِ مُطْلَقًا إذا كانَ بِشَهْوَةٍ، وإلى ما بَيْنَ السُّرَّةِ والرُّكْبَةِ إذا كانَ بِدُونِ شَهْوَةٍ›؛

و‹يَحْرُمُ› نَظَرُ العَوْراتِ ‹مِنَ الآخَرِينَ مُطْلَقًا لِغَيْرِ حاجَةٍ شَرْعِيَّةٍ›:

فَيَحْرُمُ نَظَرُ الرَّجُلِ إلى شَيْءٍ مِنْ بَدَنِ المَرْأَةِ الأَجْنَبِيَّةِ غَيْرِ الحَلِيلَةِ ‹أي غير زوجته وأمته، سِوَى الوَجْهِ والكَفَّيْنِ، ويَحْرُمُ على غَيْرِ الحَلِيلَةِ نَظَرُ ما بَيْنَ سُرَّةِ الرَّجُلِ ورُكْبَتِهِ›؛

ويَحْرُمُ عليها كَشْفُ شَيْءٍ مِنْ بَدَنِها ‹سِوَى الوَجْهِ والكَفَّيْنِ› بِحَضْرَةِ مَنْ يَحْرُمُ نَظَرُهُ إلَيْها ‹أي إلى عَوْرَتِها، وهي ما سِواهُما›،

Among the sins of the eyes are ‹men› looking at women who are not part of their unmarriageable kin ‹unconditionally, when lustful; and when looking at other than the face and hands, [even] when without lust. It is said: and when looking without lust at the face and hands except when there is a need, such as for transacting›.

It is similarly ‹unlawful› for them to look at them ‹i.e., for women to look at unrelated men, unconditionally, when lustful; and at what is between the navel and the knees, [even] when it is without lust›.

It is ‹unlawful› to look at the nakedness ‹of others, unconditionally, when there is no legal need›.

It is unlawful for a man to look at any part of a woman who is not one of his unmarriageable kin—except his lawful partner ‹i.e., except his spouse or his female slave, and other than the face and hands. It is unlawful for someone other than his lawful partner to look at what is between a man's navel and his knees›.

It is unlawful for a woman to expose any part of her body ‹other than the face and hands› in the presence of someone who cannot lawfully look at her ‹i.e., at her nakedness, which is everything other than her hands and face›.

وَيَحْرُمُ عليها وعليه ‹أي على كُلٍّ مِنَ الرَّجُلِ والمَرْأَةِ› كَشْفُ شَيْءٍ مِمّا بَيْنَ السُّرَّةِ والرُّكْبَةِ بِحَضْرَةِ مُطَّلِعٍ على العَوْراتِ، ولَوْ مَعَ ‹كَوْنِهِ مِنْ› جِنْسِـ‹ـهِ أو جِنْسِها›، ومحرميّة، غَيْرِ حَلِيلٍ،

وَيَحْرُمُ عليهما كَشْفُ السَّوْأَتَيْنِ ‹منه، وما بَيْنَ السُّرَّةِ والرُّكْبَةِ منها›، في الخَلْوَةِ لِغَيْرِ حاجَةٍ، إلّا لِحَلِيلٍ،

وحَلَّ مَعَ مَحْرَمِيَّةٍ، أو مَعَ جِنْسِيَّةٍ، أو ‹إلى› الصَّغِيرِ الَّذِي لا يُشْتَهَى ‹ولو بِلا مَحْرَمِيَّةٍ ولا جِنْسِيَّةٍ›، نَظَرُ ما عَدا ما بَيْنَ السُّرَّةِ والرُّكْبَةِ إذا كانَ بِغَيْرِ شَهْوَةٍ، إلّا ‹إلى› صَبِيٍّ وصَبِيَّةٍ دُونَ سِنِّ التَّمْيِيزِ فيَحِلُّ نَظَرُهُ ‹أي كُلِّ جِسْمِهِ›، ما عَدا فَرْجَ الأُنْثَى لِغَيْرِ أُمِّها، ‹وحَلَّ كلُّ ذلك بَيْنَ الرَّجُلِ وزَوْجَتِهِ›.

It is unlawful for her and for him ‹i.e., for both men and women› to expose anything between the navel and the knees while in the presence of someone who is aware of nakedness—even if ‹the person is› of the same sex ‹as him or her› or unmarriageable kin—except [when that person is] a lawful partner.

It is unlawful for them both «i.e., men and women» to expose the two shameful organs «the penis and buttocks» ‹for him, and between the navel and the knees for her› when in a private setting, when there is no need—except to a lawful partner.

It is permissible to look at what lies beyond the navel and the knees of [a person among one's] unmarriageable kin or the same sex, or of a minor who is not [typically] desired ‹even without being unmarriageable kin or the same sex› when done without lust. [An] except[ion is looking] at a male or female minor below the age of discernment, for it is permissible to look at them ‹i.e., all of their body›—except for a girl's private parts (except for her mother) «i.e., during the time of nursing and child-rearing, as it is permissible for her to look at it and touch it out of need. Women similar to her, such as a wet-nurse, are considered the same as her».

‹However, all of this is permissible between a man and his wife.›

وَيَحْرُمُ:

١. النَّظَرُ بِاسْتِحْقارٍ إلى مُسْلِمٍ؛
٢. والنَّظَرُ في بَيْتِ الغَيْرِ بِغَيْرِ إذْنِهِ؛
٣. أو ‹النَّظَرُ› في شَيْءٍ أَخْفاهُ كَذلك؛
٤. ومُشاهَدَةُ المُنْكَرِ ‹بِحُضُورِهِ› إذا لم يُنْكِرْ ‹بيده أو لسانه›، أو يُعذَرْ، أو لم يُفارِقْ.

The following are impermissible:

1. Looking with contempt at another Muslim.
2. Looking inside someone else's house without his permission.
3. And, likewise, ‹looking› inside something he has hidden.
4. Watching reprehensible acts ‹performed in one's presence› when he does not object [to them] ‹via his hand, or his

tongue› or «is not» excused «from doing so», or he does not depart «the scene».

THE TONGUE ‹فَصْلٌ في مَعاصِي اللِّسانِ›

ومِنْ مَعاصِي اللِّسانِ:

١. الغِيبَةُ، وهي ذِكْرُكَ أَخاكَ المُسْلِمَ ‹في خَلْفِهِ› بِما يَكْرَهُ وإنْ كانَ فيه؛
٢. والنَّمِيمَةُ، وهي نَقْلُ القَوْلِ لِلإفْسادِ؛
٣. والتَّحْرِيشُ مِنْ غَيْرِ نَقْلِ قَوْلٍ ولو بَيْنَ البَهائِمِ ‹وهو التَّحْرِيضُ على الإيذاءِ بِغَيْرِ حَقٍّ›؛
٤. والكَذِبُ ‹عَمْدًا›، و‹الكذب› هو الكَلامُ بِخِلافِ الواقِعِ؛
٥. واليَمِينُ الكاذِبَةُ ‹أي الحَلِفُ بِاسْمِ للهِ أو صِفَةٍ مِنْ صِفاتِهِ على أَمْرٍ يَعْلَمُ الحالِفُ أَنَّهُ كَذِبٌ›؛

The sins of the tongue include:

1. Backbiting [*ghībah*]. It is mentioning something about your Muslim brother ‹behind his back› that he dislikes, even if it is true.
2. Talebearing [*namīmah*]. It is repeating statements to provoke a scandal.
3. Provocation through other means—even to animals. ‹It is inciting harm without right.›
4. ‹Intentional› untruthfulness. It is speaking contrary to reality.
5. Making an untruthful oath ‹i.e., swearing an oath using the name of Allah or one of His attributes concerning some matter while the person swearing the oath knows that it is a lie›.

٦. وأَلْفاظُ القَذْفِ، وهي كَثِيرَةٌ حاصِلُها كلُّ كَلِمَةٍ تَنْسُبُ إنْسانًا أو أَحَدًا مِنْ قَرابَتِهِ إلى الزِّنا، فَهِي قَذْفٌ لمَنْ نُسِبَ الزِّنا إلَيْهِ، إمّا صَرِيحًا مُطْلَقًا، وإمّا كِنايَةً بِنِيَّةٍ، ويُحَدُّ القاذِفُ الحُرُّ ثَمانِينَ جَلْدَةً، والرقيقُ نِصْفَها؛

٧. ومنها سَبُّ ‹أَحَدِ› الصَّحابَةِ ‹أمّا سَبُّ جَمِيعِهِمْ فَهُوَ كُفْرٌ›؛

٨. وشَهادَةُ الزُّورِ؛

٩. والخُلْفُ في الوَعْدِ إذا وَعَدَهُ وهو يُضمِرُ الخُلْفَ؛

١٠. ومَطْلُ الغَنِيِّ ‹أي تَسْوِيفُهُ وتَأْخِيرُهُ وَفاءَ الدَّيْنِ الَّذِي طَلَبَهُ منه الدائِنُ مَعَ القُدْرَةِ›؛

6. Accusations of fornication. They are numerous.

The summary «of those numerous phrases» is that every phrase that asserts fornication to an individual or one of his relatives is an accusation of the person to which the fornication is attributed—unconditionally «i.e., whether intended or not» if it is explicit, or with intent if it is allusive.

An accuser who is free is flogged eighty lashes. A slave['s punishment is] half.

7. Insulting ‹one› of the companions. ‹Insulting all of them is disbelief.›
8. Perjury.
9. Violating a promise made while hiding his intent to break it.[1]
10. An affluent individual delaying payment ‹i.e., saying that he will pay in the future and delaying the payment of a debt the creditor has requested him to pay while being able to pay it›.

١١. والشَّتْمُ والسَّبُّ واللَّعْنُ ‹بِغَيْرِ حَقٍّ›؛

١٢. والاسْتِهْزاءُ بِالمُسْلِمِ؛

١٣. وكُلُّ كَلامٍ مُؤْذٍ له ‹أي لِلْمُسْلِمِ›؛

1 This section concerns sins of the tongue, so it is understood to refer to uttering a promise that one intends to break.

١٤. والكَذِبُ على اللهِ وعلى رَسُولِهِ ‹صَلَّى اللهُ عليه وسَلَّمَ، وقَدْ يَصِلانِ إلى حَدِّ الكُفْرِ›؛

١٥. والدَّعْوَى الباطِلَةُ ‹عِنْدَ قاضٍ أو غَيْرِهِ›؛

11. Disparaging, insulting, and cursing ‹without right›.
12. Mocking a Muslim.
13. Every statement injurious to him ‹i.e., a Muslim›.
14. Lying about Allah and His Messenger. ‹May Allah bless him and grant him peace. Both of these can reach the boundaries of disbelief.›
15. Making false claims ‹to a judge or anyone else›.

١٦. والطَّلاقُ البِدْعِيُّ ‹أي أثناءَ الحَيْضِ أو طُهْرٍ جامَعَها فيه›؛

١٧. والظِّهارُ ‹وهو تَشْبِيهُ زَوْجَتِهِ في الحُرْمَةِ عليه بِمَحْرَمِهِ أو عُضْوٍ منها، والمرادُ منه التَّصْرِيحُ بِالامْتِناعِ عَنْ مُجامَعَتِها أَبَدًا›، وفيه كَفَّارَةٌ إنْ لم يُطَلِّقْ فَوْرًا، وهي عِتْقُ رَقَبَةٍ مُؤْمِنَةٍ سَلِيمَةٍ، فَإِنْ عَجَزَ صامَ شَهْرَيْنِ مُتَتابِعَيْنِ، فإنْ عَجَزَ أطعم ‹أي مَلَّكَ› سِتِّينَ مِسْكِينًا سِتِّينَ مُدًّا ‹مِمّا يَصِحُ لِزَكاةِ الفِطْرِ›؛

16. Innovated divorce ‹i.e., during menstruation or a period of purity during which he has had intercourse with her›.
17. Likening one's wife to his mother [*ẓihār*]. ‹It is likening the unlawfulness of his wife—or one of her limbs—to him to one of his unmarriageable kin. What is intended is clearly expressing a refusal to ever have intercourse with her.›

    An expiation is required if there is not an immediate divorce. It «the expiation» is freeing an unblemished Muslim. If he is not able, he fasts consecutively for two months. If he is not able «to fast», he feeds ‹i.e., transfers ownership [of food] to› sixty needy individuals with one *mudd* ‹of what is suitable for Zakat al-Fiṭr›.

١٨. ومنها ‹تَعَمُّدُ› اللَّحْنِ في القُرْآنِ ‹كتغييرِ حَرَكاتِهِ› وإنْ لم يُخِلَّ بِالمَعْنَى؛
١٩. والسُّؤالُ ‹أي الشِّحاذَةُ› لِغَنِيٍّ ‹أي واجد كفايته› بِمالٍ أو حِرْفَةٍ؛
٢٠. والنَّذْرُ بِقَصْدِ إحْرامِ الوارِثِ ‹أي حِرمانِهِ مِنَ الإرْثِ›؛
٢١. وتَرْكُ الوَصِيَّةِ بَدَيْنٍ ‹لا يَعْلَمُهُ غَيْرُهُ› أو عَيْنٍ لا يَعْلَمُها غَيْرُهُ؛
٢٢. والانْتِماءُ إلى غَيْرِ أَبِيهِ أو غَيْرِ مَوالِيهِ؛
٢٣. والخِطْبَةُ على خِطْبَةِ أَخِيهِ؛
٢٤. والفَتْوَى بِغَيْرِ عِلْمٍ ‹ولو صادَفَ الصَّوابَ›؛

They «the sins of the tongue» include:

18. ‹Intentionally› mispronouncing the Quran ‹such as changing its vowels› even if it does not change the meaning.
19. Asking ‹i.e., begging› by someone who is rich ‹i.e., finds his sufficiency› due to having wealth or a trade.
20. Making a vow with the intent to bar an inheritor ‹i.e., to bar him from inheriting›.
21. Failing to make a will for a debt or an item ‹that no one else knows of›.
22. Ascribing one's lineage to someone other than one's father or [for a former slave, his affiliation] to those who freed him.
23. Seeking engagement [from a woman knowing] that his brother's engagement [has been accepted].
24. Giving fatwas without knowledge ‹even if it happens to be correct›.

٢٥. وتَعْلِيمُ وتَعلُّمُ عِلْمٍ مُضِرٍّ ‹كالسحر، لِغَيْرِ سَبَبٍ شَرْعِيٍّ›؛
٢٦. والحُكْمُ بِغَيْرِ حُكْمِ اللهِ؛
٢٧. والنَدْبُ والنِّياحَةُ؛
٢٨. وكُلُّ قَوْلٍ يَحُثُّ على مُحَرَّمٍ أو يُفَتِّرُ عن واجِبٍ؛

٢٩. وكُلُّ كَلامٍ يَقْدَحُ في الدِّينِ أو أَحَدٍ مِنَ الأَنْبياءِ أو في العُلَماءِ أو العِلْمِ ‹الشَّرْعِيِّ› أو الشَّرْعِ أو القُرْآنِ أو في شَيْءٍ مِنْ شَعائرِ اللهِ ‹وهو كُفْرٌ›؛

25. Teaching and learning harmful knowledge ‹like magic, without having a legal reason›.
26. Passing judgments that are not Allah's judgments.
27. Mournfully recounting the good deeds of the deceased and wailing over him.
28. Every statement that incites performing an unlawful act or being remiss in an obligation.
29. Every discourse denigrating the religion, one of its prophets, religious scholars, religious knowledge, the Quran, or one of Allah's rites [or where they are held «e.g., the mosque, Ṣafā and Marwah, ʿArafah, and the like» ‹which is disbelief›.

ومنها...

٣٠. التَّزْمِيرُ ‹أي العَزْفُ المُطْرِبُ على نَحْوِ المِزمارِ›؛
٣١. والسُّكُوتُ عَنِ الأَمْرِ بِالمَعْرُوفِ والنَّهْيِ عَنِ المُنْكَرِ بِغَيْرِ عُذْرٍ؛
٣٢. وكَتْمُ العِلْمِ الدِّينِيِّ الواجِبِ مَعَ وُجُودِ الطّالِبِ ‹إذا لم يُوجَدْ ذُو أَهْلِيَّةٍ لِلتَّعْلِيمِ غَيْرُهُ›؛
٣٣. والضَّحِكُ لِخُرُوجِ الرِّيحِ ‹من غيره›،
٣٤. أو ‹الضَّحِكُ› على مُسْلِمٍ اسْتِحْقارًا له؛

They [the sins of the tongue] include:

30. Playing the flute ‹i.e., melodically playing on something like a reed instrument [*mizmār*]›.
31. Inexcusably refraining from commanding the right and forbidding the wrong.

32. Withholding obligatory religious knowledge when it is requested ‹when there is no other qualified person to teach it to him›.
33. Laughing ‹at someone else› for passing wind.
34. Mockingly ‹laughing› at a Muslim.

٣٥. وكَتْمُ الشَّهادَةِ ‹إذا دُعِيَ إلَيْها، أو وَجَبَتْ عليه مِنْ غَيْرِ دَعْوَةٍ›؛

٣٦. ونِسيانُ القُرآنِ ‹وفُسِّرَ بِتَرْكِ العَمَلِ بِهِ›؛

٣٧. وتَرْكُ رَدِّ السَّلامِ الواجِبِ عَلَيْكَ؛

٣٨. والقُبْلَةُ المُحَرِّكَةُ ‹أي التَّقْبِيلُ بَيْنَ الزَّوْجَيْنِ مَعَ شَهْوَةٍ› لِلمُحْرِمِ بِنُسُكٍ ‹أي حَجٍّ أو عُمْرَةٍ›، و‹مَعَ خَشْيَةِ الإنْزالِ› لِصائمِ فَرْضٍ، أو ‹التَّقْبِيلُ مُطْلَقًا› لِمَنْ لا يَحِلُّ له قُبْلَتُه.

35. Withholding testimony ‹when one is called to provide it, or when it is obligatory to provide it without being called›.
36. Forgetting the Quran «i.e., after memorizing it». ‹It is explained [by Abū Shāmah and others] as not acting according to it [but it is not the school's official opinion].›
37. Failing to return a salutation that is obligatory to return.
38. Kissing that causes arousal ‹i.e., spouses lustfully kissing› while in the state of pilgrimage ‹i.e., Hajj or Umrah› or while fasting an obligatory fast ‹while fearing orgasm› or ‹unconditionally kissing› anyone not permissible for him to kiss.

THE EARS

فَصْلٌ ‹في مَعاصِي الأُذُنِ›

ومِنْ مَعاصِي الأُذُنِ:

١. الاسْتِماعُ إلى كَلامِ قَوْمٍ أَخْفَوْهُ عنه،

٢. و‹الاسْتِماعُ› إلى المِزمارِ والطُّنْبورِ؛ وسائرِ الأصْواتِ المُحَرَّمَةِ ‹كَسائرِ آلاتِ الطَّرَبِ النَّفْخِيَّةِ والوَتَرِيَّةِ وغَيْرِها›؛

٣. وكَالاسْتِماعِ إلى الغِيبَةِ والنَّمِيمَةِ، وسائرِ الأَقْوالِ المحَرَّمَةِ؛

٤. ‹واستماع الرجل بشهوة إلى صوت غير زوجته وأمته التي يحل له الاستمتاع بها؛ ومثله المرأة مع من لا يحل لها›.

٥. بِخِلافِ ما إذا دَخَلَ عليه السَّماعُ ‹في النقطتين السَبِقَتَيْنِ› قَهْرًا وكَرِهَهُ؛ ولَزِمَهُ الإنكارُ إنْ قَدِرَ.

The sins of the ears include:

1. Eavesdropping on a conversation that others have not made him privy to.
2. ‹Listening› to flutes, lutes, and all unlawful sounds ‹like all musical instruments that are blown, strung, or otherwise›.
3. Listening to backbiting, talebearing, and all other unlawful statements.
4. ‹A man lustfully listening to a voice that is not from his wife or a female slave he can lawfully enjoy. And similarly: a woman [listening] to someone not permissible to her.›
5. [This is] contrary to when ‹in the previous two points› one hears it involuntarily and dislikes it. He is responsible for rebuking it if able.

THE HANDS

فَصْلٌ ‹في مَعاصِي اليَدِ›

ومِنْ مَعاصِي اليَدِ:

١. التَّطْفِيفُ في الكَيْلِ والوَزْنِ والذَّرْعِ ‹أي الغِشُّ فِيها› ؛

٢. وَالسَّرِقَةُ، وَيُحَدُّ إِنْ سَرَقَ ما يُساوِي رُبْعَ دِينارٍ مِنْ حِرْزِهِ بِقَطْعِ يَدِهِ اليُمْنَى، ثُمَّ إِنْ عادَ فَرِجْلُهُ اليُسْرَى، ثُمَّ يَدُهُ اليُسْرَى، ثُمَّ رِجْلُهُ اليُمْنَى؛

The sins of the hands include:

1. Being short in measuring volumes, weights, and lengths ‹i.e., measuring them fraudulently›.
2. Theft.

There is a prescribed punishment [*ḥadd*] if he steals the equivalent of one-quarter of a dīnār from its secured location.

[The punishment is] amputating his right hand; then the left foot if he repeats; then the left hand; then the right foot.

ومنها:

٣. النَّهْبُ؛

٤. وَالغَصْبُ؛

٥. وَالمَكْسُ؛

٦. وَالغُلُولُ؛

٧. وَالقَتْلُ ‹بِغَيْرِ حَقٍّ›، وَفِيهِ الكَفَّارَةُ مُطْلَقًا ‹أي في العمد، والخَطَأِ، وشبه والخَطَأِ›، وَهِيَ عِتْقُ رَقَبَةٍ مُؤْمِنَةٍ سَلِيمَةٍ، فَإِنْ عَجَزَ صامَ شَهْرَيْنِ مُتَتَابِعَيْنِ؛ وَفِي عَمْدِهِ القِصاصُ ‹قتل القاتل› إِلَّا إِنْ عَفَى عنه ‹الوارِثُ› على الدِّيَةِ أو مجَّانًا، وَفِي الخَطَأِ وشِبْهِهِ الدِّيَةُ، وَهِيَ مِائَةٌ مِنَ الإِبِلِ فِي الذَّكَرِ الحُرِّ المُسْلِمِ، وَنِصْفُها فِي الأُنْثَى الحُرَّةِ المُسْلِمَةِ، وَتَخْتَلِفُ صِفاتُ الدِّيَةِ بِحَسَبِ القَتْلِ؛

They «the sins of the hands» include:

3. Plundering.
4. Wrongfully taking [rights or property] through force.
5. Tax collection.

6. Stealing from the spoils of war.
7. Killing ‹without right›.

   There is an unconditional expiation for it ‹i.e., in deliberate, accidental, and quasi-accidental killings›. It is freeing an unblemished Muslim slave. If unable, one consecutively fasts for two months.

   When the killing is deliberate, there is a reciprocal punishment [*qiṣāṣ*] ‹i.e., the killer is killed› unless ‹an inheritor› forgoes it for blood-money [*al-diyah*] or for free.

   When the killing is accidental and quasi-accidental, there is blood-money. It is one-hundred camels for [killing] a free Muslim male; and half of that for a free Muslim female.

   The qualities of the blood-money depend upon the killing.

ومنها:

٨. الضَّرْبُ بِغَيْرِ حَقٍّ؛

٩. وأَخْذُ الرَّشْوَةِ ‹مطلقًا›؛

١٠. وإعْطاؤُها ‹أي الرَّشْوَةِ إلّا إذا اضْطُرَّ إليها لِتَحْصِيلِ حَقٍّ أو دَفْعِ ظُلْمٍ›؛

١١. وإحْراقُ الحَيَوانِ ‹حيًّا› إلّا إذا آذَى وتَعَيَّنَ طَرِيقًا في الدَّفْعِ؛

١٢. والمُثْلَةُ بِالحَيَوانِ ‹أي تعذيبه بنحو تَقْطِيعِهِ حَيًّا›؛

١٣. واللَّعِبُ بِالنَّرْدِ، والطابِ ‹ونحوهما مما يعتمد على الحرز والتخمين›،

١٤. و‹اللَّعِبُ بِـ› كُلِّ ما فيه قِمارٌ، حَتَّى لَعِبُ الصِّبْيانِ بالجَوْزِ والكِعابِ ‹لا يَجُوزُ أَنْ يُؤْذَنَ لهم به إنْ كانَ على وَجْهٍ مُحَرَّمٍ›؛

١٥. واللّهْوُ ‹أي العَزْفُ المُطْرِبُ› بِآلاتِ اللَّهْوِ ‹أي المُوسِيقا› المُحَرَّمَةِ كَالطُّنْبُورِ والرَّبابِ والمِزمارِ والأَوْتارِ؛

They «the sins of the hands» include:

8. Striking without right.
9. Taking bribes ‹unconditionally›.
10. Giving them ‹i.e., bribes, unless one is forced to do so in order to obtain a right or repel a harm›.
11. Burning ‹a living› animal unless it is aggressive and that is the only way to repel it.
12. Mutilating an animal ‹i.e., torturing it by cutting it while alive or the like›.
13. Playing cribbage and *ṭāb*.[2] ‹And similar games that rely upon chance and speculation.›
14. ‹Playing› anything involving gambling—even boys playing with walnuts «or coconuts» and play-bones [or dice]. ‹It is not permissible to allow them to play it when it is in an unlawful manner.›
15. Amusement ‹i.e., emotional melodies› via entertaining ‹i.e., musical› instruments which are unlawful, like *ṭunbūr* [a type of two-string lyre], *rabāb* [a type of one-stringed lute], flutes, and [other] stringed instruments.

١٦. ولمَسُ ‹الرجل› الأَجْنَبِيَّةِ ‹أي غَيْرِ زَوْجَتِهِ وأَمَتِه ومَحرَمِهِ› عَمْدًا بِغَيْرِ حائِلٍ ‹مطلقًا ولو لمصاحفة›،

١٧. أو به ‹أي الحائل› بِشَهْوَةٍ ‹بين غير نحو الزوجين› ولَوْ مَعَ جِنْسٍ أو مَحْرَمِيَّةٍ؛

١٨. وتَصْوِيرُ الحَيوانِ ‹أي مُحاكاةُ وتمثيل الشكل لِذِي رُوحٍ بالرسم أو النحت أو غيرهما، سَواءٌ كانَ بِحَجْمٍ أم بِدُونِهِ، سِوَى دُمْيَةِ البِنْتِ الصَّغِيرَةِ›؛

2 A game of chance that used to be popular and well-known.

١٩. ومَنْعُ الزَّكاةِ أو بَعْضِها، بَعْدَ الوُجُوبِ والتَّمَكُّنِ، أو إخْراجُ ما لا يُجْزِئُ، أو إعْطاؤُها مَنْ لا يَسْتَحِقُّها ‹كَإِنْفاقِها في بِناءِ المساجِدِ فيحرم ولا يجزئ›؛

٢٠. ومَنْعُ الأَجِيرِ أُجْرَتَهُ؛

٢١. ومَنْعُ المُضْطَرِّ ‹المَعْصُومِ الدَّمِ› ما يَسُدُّهُ ‹أي ما يُنْقِذُهُ مِنَ الهَلاكِ›؛

٢٢. وعَدَمُ إنْقاذِ غَرِيقٍ ‹مَعْصُومِ الدَّمِ›، مِنْ غَيْرِ عُذْرٍ فيهما ‹أي هذِهِ والَّتِي قَبْلَها›؛

٢٣. وكِتابَةُ ما يَحْرُمُ النُّطْقُ بِه؛

٢٤. والخِيانَةُ، وهي ضِدُّ النَّصِيحَةِ، فَتَشْمَلُ الأَفْعالَ والأَقْوالَ والأَحْوالَ.

16. ‹A man› touching an unrelated woman ‹i.e., not his wife, female slave, or unmarriageable kin›, intentionally and without a barrier ‹unconditionally—even to shake hands›.
17. [Touching] lustfully with one ‹i.e., a barrier, when not between spouses›—even when it is with the same sex or [one's] kin.
18. Depicting an animal ‹i.e., simulating and representing the form of an ensouled creature via drawing, carving, or other means, whether it is to scale or smaller, except for a young girl's doll›.
19. Withholding zakat or part of it after it becomes due and one is able to pay it, or extracting what does not fulfill [the requisite conditions], or giving it to someone who does not deserve it ‹like spending it in building mosques—for this is unlawful and does not fulfill›.
20. Withholding an employee's wages.
21. Withholding something from someone ‹whose life is protected› in dire need that would alleviate his hunger ‹i.e., what saves him from death›.

22. Failing to rescue someone drowning ‹whose life is protected› without an excuse in these two ‹i.e., this one and the preceding one›.
23. Writing what is unlawful to utter.
24. Deceit. It is the opposite of honesty. It includes actions, statements, and attitudes.

THE PRIVATE PARTS

فَصْلٌ ‹في مَعاصِي الفَرْجِ›

ومِنْ مَعاصِي الفَرْجِ:

٢٥. الزِّنا واللِّواطُ، ويُحَدُّ ‹بالزِّنا› الحُرُّ المُحْصَنُ، ذَكَرًا أو أُنْثَى، بِالرَّجْمِ بِالحِجارَةِ المُعْتَدِلَةِ حَتَّى يَمُوتَ، وغَيْرُهُ ‹أي غَيْرُ المُحْصَنِ› بِمِائَةِ جَلْدَةٍ وتَغْرِيبِ سَنَةٍ لِلحُرِّ، ونِصْفِ ذلك لِلرَّقِيقِ؛ ‹وحدّ فاعل اللواط كحدّ الزنا›؛

The sins of the private parts include:

1. Fornication and anal sex.

The prescribed punishment ‹for fornication› for someone who has the capacity to remain chaste ‹[*muḥṣan*]›—whether male or female—is being pelted with moderately sized stones until death. For others ‹i.e., those lacking the capacity to remain chaste›, it is one hundred lashings and banishment for one year for a free person and a half [of that] for a slave.

‹The prescribed punishment for performing anal sex is the same as the prescribed punishment for fornication.›

ومنها:

٢٦. ‹أي معاصي الفرج، شُذُوذُ› إتْيانِ البَهائِمِ ولو مِلْكَهُ، ‹ويعاقبه الخليفة بما يراه›؛

٢٧. والاسْتِمْناءُ ‹أي اسْتِدْعاءُ خُرُوجِ المَنِيِّ› بِيَدِ غَيْرِ الحَلِيلَةِ ‹أي الزَّوْجَةِ والأَمَةِ الَّتِي تَحِلُّ له›؛

٢٨. والوَطْءُ في الحَيْضِ، أو النِّفاسِ، أو بَعْدَ انْقِطاعِهِما وقَبْلَ الغُسْلِ، أو بَعْدَ غُسْلٍ بِلا نِيَّةٍ ‹مِنَ المُغْتَسِلَةِ›، أَوْ مَعَ فَقْدِ شَرْطٍ مِنْ شُرُوطِهِ؛

٢٩. والتَّكَشُّفُ ‹أي كشف الْعَوْرَةِ› عِنْدَ مَنْ يَحْرُمُ نَظَرُهُ إليهـ‹ا›، أو ‹السوأتين للرجل وما بين السرّة والركبة للحرة› في خَلْوَةٍ لِغَيْرِ غَرَضٍ ‹كَاغْتِسالٍ أو تَبَرُّدٍ أو تَمَتُّعِ زَوْجٍ›،

They ‹i.e., sins of the private parts› include:

2. ‹The perversion of› bestiality—even if they are his property. ‹The Caliph punishes him however he sees fit.›
3. Masturbation. [It is] ‹inducing ejaculation› using the hand of a non-lawful partner «“lawful partner” meaning his wife or a female slave who is lawful to him».
4. Intercourse during menstruation, postpartum bleeding, or after they have ended but before bathing, or after bathing but without any intention ‹from the one bathing›, or when one of its conditions are missing.
5. Exposure ‹i.e., exposing one’s nakedness› in the presence of someone who cannot lawfully look at it, or, when alone in a private spot, without any purpose ‹like for washing, or cooling down, or the spouse’s enjoyment›.

٣٠. واسْتِقْبالُ القِبْلَةِ أو اسْتِدْبارُها بِبَوْلٍ أو غائِطٍ مِنْ غَيْرِ حائِلٍ ‹كَجِدارٍ في جهة القبلة يستتر به›، أو كانَ وبَعُدَ عنه أَكْثَرَ مِنْ ثَلاثَةِ أَذْرُعٍ، أو كانَ أَقَلَّ مِنْ ثُلُثَيْ ذِراعٍ، إلّا في المُعَدِّ لِذلك؛

٣١. والتَّغَوُّطُ ‹والتبَوُّلُ› على القَبْرِ،

٣٢. و‹التَّغَوُّطُ و›البَوْلُ في المَسْجِدِ ولَوْ في إناءٍ،

٣٣. و‹التَّغَوُّطُ والبَوْلُ› على المُعَظَّمِ ‹وهُوَ كُفْرٌ على نحو المُصْحَفِ مَهْما كانَ مُرادُهُ›،

٣٤. وتَرْكُ الخِتانِ بَعْدَ البُلُوغِ ‹ولا يَحْرُمُ على وَجْهٍ›.

6. Facing the direction of prayer or turning one's back to it while urinating or defecating without using a barrier ‹like a wall in the direction of the prayer that conceals him›, or there is [a barrier] but he is further than three *dhirā*'s [144 centimeters or 56.7 inches] away from it, or it is lower than two-thirds of a dhirā' in height [32 centimeters or 12.6 inches]—except in a lavatory.
7. Defecating ‹and urinating› on a grave.
8. ‹Defecating and› urinating in the masjid—even into a container.
9. ‹Defecating and urinating› on something that is venerated. ‹It is disbelief when done on something like a *muṣḥaf*—regardless of the intent.›
10. Failing to circumcise after reaching maturity. ‹It is not unlawful according to one *wajh*.[3]›

---

3 A *wajh* is an opinion issued by one of the early Shāfi'ī scholars.

THE LEGS

فَصْلٌ ‹في مَعاصِي الرِّجْلِ›

ومِنْ مَعاصِي الرِّجْلِ:

١. المَشْيُ في مَعْصِيَةٍ، كَالمَشْيِ في سِعايَةٍ بِمُسْلِمٍ أو قَتْلِهِ أو فِيما يَضُرُّهُ بِغَيْرِ حَقٍّ ‹ولو لم يَفْعَلْ ما مَشَى إلَيْهِ›؛

٢. وإِباقُ ‹أيْ هَرَبُ› العَبْدِ ‹مِنْ سَيِّدِهِ› والزَّوْجَةِ ‹مِنْ زَوْجِها›، ومَنْ عليه حَقٌّ عَمّا يَلْزَمُه مِنْ قِصاصٍ أو دَيْنٍ أو نَفَقَةٍ أو بِرِّ والِدٍ أو تَرْبِيَةِ أَطْفالٍ؛

٣. والتَّبَخْتُرُ في المَشْيِ ‹أيْ المَشْيُ بِكِبْرٍ وخُيَلاءَ وتَعاظُمٍ›؛

٤. وتَخَطِّي الرِّقابِ إلّا لفُرْجَةٍ؛

٥. والمُرُورُ بَيْنَ يَدَيِ المُصَلِّي إذا كَمَلَتْ شُرُوطُ سُتْرَتِهِ،

The sins of the legs include:

1. Walking to commit an act of disobedience, like walking to defame a Muslim, kill him, or harm him without right ‹even if one does not carry out what he walked there to do›.
2. A slave fleeing ‹i.e., running away from his master›, a wife ‹from her husband›, or whoever owes a right running from his responsibility (like a reciprocal punishment, debt, support, obeying a parent, or raising a child).
3. Strutting ‹i.e., walking with arrogance, conceit, and pride›.
4. Stepping over people—unless it is to reach an empty space.
5. Passing in front of someone while they are praying when they have fulfilled the conditions for placing a barrier.

٦. ومَدُّ الرِّجْلِ إلى المُصْحَفِ إذا كانَ غَيْرَ مُرْتَفِعٍ ‹عن مستوى القدم، ولم يَكُنْ في خِزانَةٍ مَرْدُودَةِ البابِ أو خَلْفَ حائِلٍ›؛

٧. وكُلُّ مَشْيٍ إلى مُحَرَّمٍ؛

٨. أو ‹كُلُّ› تَخَلُّفٍ عن واجِبٍ.

6. Extending one's legs to the Quran when it is not raised up ‹above foot-level and is not within a closed-door cabinet or behind a barrier›.
7. Walking to something unlawful «like walking to a tyrant's door».
8. ‹Any› walking away from an obligation.

THE BODY

فَصْلٌ ‹في مَعاصِي البَدَنِ›

ومِنْ مَعاصِي البَدَنِ:

١. عُقُوقُ الوالِدَيْنِ ‹وما دُونَهُ مِنْ إيذائِهِما›؛

٢. والفِرارُ مِنَ الزَّحْفِ ‹أي الهَرَبُ مِنْ بَيْنِ المُقاتِلِينَ في سَبِيلِ اللهِ بَعْدَ الحُضُورِ معهم في مَوْضِعِ القِتالِ›؛

٣. وقَطِيعَةُ الرَّحِمِ؛

٤. وإيذاءُ الجارِ، ولو كافِرًا له أمانٌ، إيذاءً ظاهِرًا؛

٥. والاخْتِضابُ ‹أي صبغ الشَّعْرِ› بِالسَّوادِ؛

The sins of the body include:

1. Ingratitude towards one's parents ‹and lesser annoyances›.
2. Fleeing from battle ‹i.e., running away from amongst those fighting in the path of Allah after being present with them in the place of battle›.
3. Severing family ties.
4. Annoying neighbors (even a disbeliever who has safe-conduct) with an obvious annoyance.
5. Dyeing ‹i.e., coloring the hair› black.

٦. وتَشَبُّهُ الرِّجالِ بِالنِّساءِ وعَكْسُهُ ‹في المَلْبَسِ وغَيْرِهِ›؛

٧. وَإِسْبَالُ الثَّوْبِ لِلْخُيَلاءِ ‹أَيْ تَطْوِيلُ الثَّوْبِ إِلى ما دُونَ رُسْغِ القَدَمِ تَكَبُّرًا وَبَطَرًا›؛

٨. وَالحِنّاءُ في اليَدَيْنِ وَالرِّجْلَيْنِ لِلرَّجُلِ بِلا حاجَةٍ؛

٩. وَقَطْعُ الفَرْضِ بِغَيْرِ عُذْرٍ؛

١٠. وَقَطْعُ ‹ما شرع فيه من› نَفْلِ الحَجِّ وَالعُمْرَةِ ‹بِغَيْرِ عُذْرٍ›؛

6. Men imitating women and the opposite ‹in clothing and other things›.
7. Dragging one's garment out of conceit ‹i.e., lengthening the garment below the ankle out of arrogance and hubris›.
8. A man applying henna to the hands and feet without need.
9. Interrupting an obligation «e.g., a prayer or fast» without an excuse.
10. Interrupting a voluntary Hajj or Umrah ‹after initiating it, without an excuse›.

١١. وَمُحاكاةُ المُؤْمِنِ ‹وهو المُسْلِمُ، بِأَنْ يَأْتِيَ بِمِثْلِ قوله أو فعله› اسْتِهْزاءً بِهِ؛

١٢. وَالتَّجَسُّسُ ‹أَيِ التَّتَبُّعُ وَالبَحْثُ› عَلى عَوْراتِ النّاسِ ‹أَي عُيُوبِهِمْ›؛

١٣. وَالوَشْمُ؛

١٤. وَهَجْرُ المُسْلِمِ فَوْقَ ثَلاثـ‹ةِ أَيّامٍ› لِغَيْرِ عُذْرٍ شَرْعِيٍّ؛

١٥. وَمُجالَسَةُ المُبْتَدِعِ وَالفاسِقِ لِلإِيناسِ ‹له على ضَلالِهِ›؛

11. Making an impression of a believer ‹who is a Muslim, by imitating his statements and actions› to mock him.
12. Spying on ‹i.e., investigating and seeking out› what people keep secret ‹i.e., their defects›.
13. Tattooing.
14. Shunning a Muslim for more than three ‹days› without a legal reason.

15. Engaging in social intercourse with someone who is an innovator or morally corrupt to be amicable ‹towards him in spite of his misguidance›.

١٦. ولُبْسُ الذَّهَبِ، والفِضَّةِ، والحَرِيرِ أو ما أَكْثَرُهُ وَزْنًا منه ‹أي الحرير›، لِلرَّجُلِ البالِغِ، إلّا خاتَمَ الفِضَّةِ؛

١٧. والخَلْوَةُ بِالأَجْنَبِيَّةِ ‹أي غَيْرِ المَحْرَمِ، إن لم تكن زَوْجَتَهُ ولا ملك يمينه›؛

١٨. وسَفَرُ المَرْأَةِ ‹لِغَيْرِ عذر› بِغَيْرِ نَحْوِ مَحْرَمٍ ‹كزوج›؛

١٩. واسْتِخْدامُ الحُرِّ كُرْهًا ‹أي سُخْرَةً›؛

٢٠. والاسْتِخْفافُ بِالعُلَماءِ ‹الشَّرْعِيِّينَ، وهو كفر إن كان بجميعهم›،

16. Wearing gold, silver, silk, or [clothing when] the majority of its weight is from it ‹i.e., silk›—for mature men—except for a silver ring.
17. Being alone with a woman who is not related to him ‹i.e., who is not one's unmarriageable kin [*maḥram*] if she is not his wife or his slave›.
18. A woman traveling ‹without an excuse› without the likes of one's unmarriageable kin ‹like a spouse›.
19. Employing a freeman forcibly ‹i.e., to do something he has no desire to perform›.
20. Contempt for scholars ‹of religion. It is disbelief when it is for them all.›

٢١. و‹الاسْتِخْفافُ› بِالإمامِ ‹أي الخَلِيفَةِ› العادِلِ،

٢٢. و‹الاسْتِخْفافُ› بِالشائبِ المُسْلِمِ؛

٢٣. ومُعاداةُ الوَلِيِّ؛

٢٤. والإعانَةُ ‹ولو لكافر› على المَعْصِيَةِ؛

٢٥. وتَرْوِيجُ الزّائِفِ ‹كالعملة المزوّرة›؛

21. ‹Contempt› for a just Imām ‹i.e., the Caliph›.
22. ‹Contempt› for elderly Muslims.
23. Enmity towards a *walī* ‹friend of Allah›.
24. Assisting another ‹even a disbeliever› in disobedience.
25. Circulating counterfeit coins ‹i.e., like counterfeit currency›.

٢٦. واسْتِعْمالُ أَوانِي الذَّهَبِ والفِضَّةِ واتِّخاذُها ‹أي اقْتِناؤُها لِغَيْرِ اسْتِعمالٍ›؛
٢٧. وتَرْكُ الفَرْضِ، أو فِعْلُهُ مَعَ تَرْكِ رُكْنٍ له أو شَرْطٍ، أو مَعَ فِعْلِ مُبْطِلٍ له؛
٢٨. وتَرْكُ الجُمُعَةِ مَعَ وُجُوبِها عليه وإنْ صَلَّى الظُّهْرَ؛
٢٩. وتَرْكُ نَحْوِ أَهْلِ قَرْيَةٍ الجَماعَةَ في المَكْتُوباتِ ‹أي الصَّلَواتِ المَفْرُوضَةِ›؛
٣٠. وتَأْخِيرُ الفَرْضِ عَنْ وَقْتِهِ بِغَيْرِ عُذْرٍ؛

26. Using gold and silver implements and acquiring them ‹i.e., possessing them without using them›.
27. Failing to perform any obligation or performing it without one of its essential elements or conditions, or performing it with an invalidator.
28. Failing to perform Friday Prayer when it is obligatory for him—even if he prayed the Noon Prayer.
29. A village (or its like) failing to congregate for obligatory prayers.
30. Delaying an obligation beyond its time without an excuse.

٣١. ورَمْيُ الصَّيْدِ بِالمُثَقَّلِ المُذَفِّفِ ‹أي ما يَقْتُلُ بِثِقْلِهِ كَالحَجَرِ›؛
٣٢. واتِّخاذُ الحَيوانِ غَرَضًا ‹أي هَدَفًا لِلرِّمايَةِ بدون مسوّغ شرعيّ›؛
٣٣. وعَدَمُ مُلازَمَةِ المُعْتَدَّةِ لِلْمَسْكَنِ بِغَيْرِ عُذْرٍ؛
٣٤. وعَدَمُ الإحْدادِ على الزَّوْجِ ‹المُتَوَفَّى›؛
٣٥. وتَنْجِيسُ المَسْجِدِ، وتَقْذِيرُه ولو بِطاهِرٍ؛

31. Hunting prey using blunt objects ‹i.e., what kills through its force—like a stone›.

32. Using an animal as a target ‹i.e., a target for marksmanship, without a legal justification›.
33. A woman leaving the house during her waiting period without an excuse.
34. Forgoing mourning ‹[iḥdād]› for a ‹deceased› husband.
35. Making a mosque filthy or soiling it—even with something pure.

٣٦. وَالتَّهَاوُنُ بِالحَجِّ بَعْدَ الاسْتِطَاعَةِ إِلى أَنْ يَمُوتَ؛

٣٧. وَالاسْتِدانَةُ لِمَنْ لا يَرْجُو وَفاءً لِدَيْنِهِ مِنْ جِهَةٍ ظاهِرَةٍ ولم يَعْلَمْ دائِنُهُ ‹أي مقرضه› بذلك؛

٣٨. وعَدَمُ انْظارِ المُعْسِرِ ‹عن وفاء الدين›؛

٣٩. وبَذْلُ المالِ ‹أي صرفه› في مَعْصِيَةٍ؛

٤٠. والاسْتِهانَةُ بِالمُصْحَفِ ‹وهي كُفْرٌ إِنْ كانَتْ نَحْوَ رَمْيِهِ في القَذَرِ، ومَعْصِيَةٌ دُونَ الكُفْرِ إِنْ كانَتْ نَحْوَ مَسِّهِ بِلا وُضُوءٍ›،

36. Delaying Hajj, after one was able to perform it, until death.
37. Borrowing for someone who has no expectation of repaying his debt from an apparent means while his lender ‹i.e., his creditor› is unaware.
38. Not allowing someone lacking the funds ‹to fulfill his debt› to defer payment «to when he is able».
39. Wasting money ‹i.e., spending it› in disobedience.
40. Disdaining the Quran. ‹It is disbelief if it is through the likes of throwing it into something foul. It is disobedience that is less than disbelief if it is through the likes of touching it without ablution.›

٤١. و‹الاسْتِهانَةُ› بِكُلِّ عِلْمٍ شَرْعِيٍّ ‹وهي كُفْرٌ إنْ كانَتْ بِمَعْنَى الاسْتِخْفافِ، ومَعْصِيَةٌ لَيْسَتْ كُفْرًا إن كانَتْ بِمَعْنَى ما يُشْعِرُ بِمُجَرَّدِ الإخْلالِ بِواجِبِ التَّعْظِيمِ›؛

٤٢. وتَمْكِينُ الصَّبِيِّ غَيْرِ المُميِّزِ منه ‹أي المُصْحَفِ مُطْلَقًا، والمُمَيِّزِ لِغَيْرِ الدِّراسَةِ›؛

٤٣. وتَغْيِيرُ مَنارِ الأَرْضِ؛

٤٤. أو التَّصَرُّفُ في الشّارِعِ بِما لا يَجُوزُ ‹كأنْ يَسُدَّهُ أو يَضَعَ فيه ما يَضُرُّ بِالمارَّةِ›؛

٤٥. واسْتِعْمالُ المُعارِ في غَيْرِ المَأْذُونِ فيه؛ أو زادَ على المُدَّةِ المَأْذُونِ له فِيها؛ أو أَعارَهُ لِغَيْرِهِ ‹بِلا إذْنٍ›؛

41. ‹Disdain› for all religious sciences. ‹It is disbelief when it has the meaning of contempt. It is an act of disobedience that is not disbelief when it has the meaning of something that feels like simply violating the obligation of reverance.›
42. Allowing a youth without discernment access to it ‹i.e., the Quran, unconditionally. And allowing one with discernment for reasons other than study›.
43. Tampering with property markers.
44. Using the street in an impermissible manner ‹like blocking it, or placing something harmful to those passing through›.
45. Using a lent item in an unauthorized manner, exceeding the duration he is authorized to use it, or lending it to someone else ‹without authorization›.

٤٦. وتَحْجِيرُ المُباحِ، كَالمَرْعَى والاحْتِطابِ مِنَ المَواتِ ‹أي الأَرْضِ الَّتِي لا يَمْلِكُها إنْسانٌ›، والمِلْحِ مِنْ مَعْدِنِهِ ‹أي مَنْجَمِهِ›، والنَّقْدَيْنِ وغَيْرِهِما، والماءِ لِلشُّرْبِ مِنَ المُسْتَخْلَفِ؛

٤٧. واسْتِعْمالُ اللُّقَطَةِ قَبْلَ التَّمَلُّكِ ‹الَّذي يَلِي التَّعْريفَ› بِشُرُوطِهِ؛

٤٨. والجُلُوسُ ‹في مَكانِ المَعْصِيَةِ› مَعَ مُشاهَدَةِ المُنْكَرِ ‹أي العِلْمِ بِهِ› إذا لم يُعْذَرْ؛

٤٩. والتَّطَفُّلُ في الوَلائِمِ، وهو الدُّخُولُ بِغَيْرِ إذْنٍ أو ‹إذا› أَدْخَلُوهُ حَياءً؛

٥٠. وأَنْ ‹يَكُونَ الشخص ممن› يُكْرِمُـ‹ـه› المَرْءُ اتِّقاءَ لِشَرِّهِ؛

46. Blocking access to public resources—like pasture and wood-gathering on unclaimed lands ‹i.e., lands not owned by any individual›, salt from its mine ‹i.e., its quarry› and gold, silver, and other [metals and minerals], and drinking water from a renewable source.
47. Using a lost item «that one has found» before taking ownership of it ‹which is preceded by announcing it› according to its conditions.
48. Sitting ‹in a place of disobedience› and observing what is objectionable ‹i.e., having knowledge of it› while one is not excused.
49. Sponging at feasts. It is entering them without authorization or being allowed entry out of shame.
50. ‹Being a person› others ‹must› honor in order to be safeguarded from his wickedness.

٥١. وعَدَمُ التَّسْوِيَةِ بَيْنَ الزَّوْجاتِ ‹في النَّفَقَةِ والمَبيتِ›؛

٥٢. وخُرُوجُ المَرْأَةِ مُتَعَطِّرَةً أو مُتَزَيِّنَةً، ولَوْ مَسْتُورَةً وبِإذْنِ زَوْجِها، إذا كانَتْ تَمُرُّ على رِجالٍ أجانِبَ ‹بِقَصْدِ اسْتِمالَتِهِمْ إلَيْها، وإلا كُرِه›؛

٥٣. والسِّحْرُ ‹ولو لِفَكِّ سِحْرٍ أو لِتَحْبِيبٍ›؛

٥٤. والخُرُوجُ عَنْ طاعَةِ الإمامِ ‹أي الخَليفَةِ›؛

٥٥. والتَّوَلِّي على يَتِيمٍ أو مَسْجِدٍ أو لِقَضاءٍ ونَحْوِ ذلك مَعَ عِلْمِهِ بِالعَجْزِ عَنِ القِيامِ بِتِلْكَ الوَظِيفَةِ؛

51. Not giving equal treatment to wives ‹in support and cohabitation›.
52. A woman going out while perfumed or dressed up (even if she is covered and with her husband's permission) if she will pass by unrelated men ‹with the intent of causing them to incline towards her. Otherwise, it is offensive›.
53. Magic ‹even to undo magic or cause love›.
54. Rebelling against the Imām ‹i.e., the Caliph›.
55. Accepting guardianship over an orphan or mosque, or a judgeship and the like, while he knows that he is unable to execute those functions.

٥٦. وإيواءُ الظّالِمِ ومَنْعُهُ ‹أي حِمايَتُهُ› مِمَّنْ يُرِيدُ أَخْذَ الحَقِّ منه؛

٥٧. وتَرْوِيعُ المُسْلِمِينَ ‹أي إخافَتُهُمْ›؛

٥٨. وقَطْعُ الطَّرِيقِ، ويُحَدُّ ‹أي يُعاقَبُ› بِحَسَبِ جِنايَتِهِ، إمّا بِتَعْزِيرٍ ‹إنْ أَخافَ السَّبِيلَ فَقَطْ›، أو بِقَطْعِ يَدٍ ورِجْلٍ مِنْ خِلافٍ ‹إنْ أخافَ وأَخَذَ المالَ ولم يَقْتُلْ›، أو بِقَتْلٍ ‹إن أخاف وقتل ولم يأخذ المال›، أو بِقَتْلٍ وصَلْبٍ ‹إنْ أخافَ وأَخَذَ المالَ وقَتَلَ›؛

56. Sheltering a wrong-doer and protecting him ‹i.e., giving him refuge› from someone seeking to obtain his right from him.
57. Terrorizing Muslims ‹i.e., frightening them›.
58. Highway robbery. He is punished according to his crime with either:
    - A disciplinary punishment ‹if he only spread fear along the path›.
    - Amputating the opposite hand and foot ‹if he spread fear and took property but did not kill›.
    - Execution ‹if he spread fear and killed but without taking property›.
    - Execution and crucifixion ‹if he spread fear, took property, and killed›.

ومنها:

٥٩. عَدَمُ الوَفاءِ بِالنَّذْرِ؛

٦٠. والوِصالُ في الصَّوْمِ ‹عَمْدًا بِغَيْرِ عُذْرٍ›؛

٦١. وأَخْذُ مَجْلِسِ غَيْرِهِ ‹في نَحْوِ مَسْجِدٍ›، أو زَحْمَتُهُ المُؤْذِيَةُ، أو أَخْذُ نَوْبَتِهِ.

٦٢. ‹والتضامّ، ولو بحائل ودون شهوة، عند اختلاف الجنس، وعدم نحو الزوجيّة، وعدم المحرميّة، ولو بين الرجل وخطيبته قبل العقد›.

The sins of the body include:

59. Failing to fulfill a sworn vow.
60. Fasting without interruption ‹intentionally, and without an excuse›.
61. Occupying someone else's seat ‹such as in a mosque›, harmfully crowding them, or taking their turn.
62. ‹Being in close physical proximity—even with a barrier and without lust—when there is a mix of sexes without something like marriage or kinship—even a man and his fiancée before the marriage contract.›

REPENTANCE

فَصْلٌ ‹في التَّوْبَةِ›

تَجِبُ التَّوْبَةُ مِنَ الذُّنُوبِ ‹صَغِيرِها وكَبِيرِها› فَوْرًا على كُلِّ مُكَلَّفٍ، وهي:

١. النَّدَمُ،

٢. والإِقْلاعُ،

٣. والعَزْمُ على أنْ لا يَعُودَ إِلَيْها،

٤. و‹لا يُشْتَرَطُ› الاسْتِغْفارُ ‹بِاللِّسانِ›،

٥. وإنْ كانَ الذَّنْبُ تَرْكَ فَرْضٍ قَضاهُ، أو تَبِعَةً لِآدَمِيٍّ قَضاهُ أو اسْتَرْضاهُ.

Repentance from ‹minor and major› sins is required, immediately, from every responsible individual. It is:

1. Regretting «the act».
2. Cessation «from the sin».
3. Resolving to not repeat it.
4. Seeking forgiveness. ‹Uttering it is not a condition.›
5. If the sin is failing to perform an obligation, he performs it. Or [if the sin] is a liability to a human, he performs it or placates him.

AUTHOR'S CLOSING REMARKS

خاتِمَةُ المؤلّف

انْتَهَى ما قَدَّرَ اللهُ جَمْعَه، وأَرْجُو منه سُبْحانَهُ أنْ يُعِمَّ نَفْعَه، ويُكثِرَ في القُلُوبِ وَقْعَه، وأَطْلُبُ مِمَّنِ اطَّلَعَ عليه مِنْ أُولِي المَعْرِفَةِ ورَأَى فيه خَطَأً أو زَلَلاً أنْ يُنَبِّهَ على ذٰلك، بِالرَّدِّ الصَّرِيحِ، لِيَحْذَرَ النَّاسُ مِنَ اتِّباعِي على غَيْرِ الصَّوابِ، فَالحَقُّ أَحَقُّ أنْ يُتَّبَعَ، والإنْسانُ مَحَلُّ الخَطَأِ والنِّسْيانِ.

﴿رَبَّنَا اغْفِرْ لَنَا وَلِإِخْوَانِنَا الَّذِينَ سَبَقُونَا بِالإِيمَانِ وَلا تَجْعَلْ فِي قُلُوبِنَا غِلًّا لِلَّذِينَ ءامَنُوا رَبَّنَا إِنَّكَ رَءُوفٌ رَحِيمٌ﴾،

اللّٰهُمَّ مَغْفِرَتُكَ أَوْسَعُ مِنْ ذُنُوبِنا، ورَحْمَتُكَ أَرْجَى عِنْدَنا مِنْ أَعْمالِنا،

﴿سُبْحَانَ رَبِّكَ رَبِّ الْعِزَّةِ عَمَّا يَصِفُونَ * وَسَلامٌ عَلَى الْمُرْسَلِينَ * وَالْحَمْدُ للهِ رَبِّ الْعَالَمِينَ﴾ - آمِينَ.

قالَ مُؤَلِّفُهُ، سَيِّدُنا الحَبِيبُ عَبْدُ اللهِ بْنُ الحُسَيْنِ بْنِ طاهِرٍ عَلَوِيٌّ رَضِيَ اللهُ عنه: وكانَ الفَراغُ مِنْ إمْلائِهِ فاتِحَةَ رَجَبٍ، سَنَةَ أَلْفٍ ومِائَتَيْنِ وإحْدَى وأَرْبَعِين، وصَلَّى اللهُ على سَيِّدِنا مُحَمَّدٍ وآلِهِ وصَحْبِهِ وسَلَّمَ

[This] finishes what Allah destined to be compiled. I hope that He—Glorified is He—will spread its benefit, and make much of it stick in hearts. I ask anyone knowledgeable who examines it and sees an error or a slip to point it out by explicitly noting it «by saying it or writing it in the margin» in order to warn people from following me in what is not correct. For truth is more rightful to be followed, and people are prone to mistakes and forgetfulness.

"Our Lord! forgive us and those of our brethren who had precedence of us in faith, and do not allow any spite to remain in our hearts towards those who believe, our Lord! surely Thou art Kind, Merciful" (Q59:10).

O, Allah! Your forgiveness is vaster than our sins, and your mercy is more hopeful to us than our own actions.

"Glory be to your Lord, the Lord of Honor, above what they describe * And peace be on the messengers. * And all praise is due to Allah, the Lord of the worlds." (Q37:180–82). Āmīn!

Its author, our master al-Ḥabīb 'Abd Allāh bin al-Ḥusayn bin Ṭāhir 'Alawī (may Allah be pleased with him) said: "I finished its dictation at the beginning of Rajab, 1241 AH [February, 1826 CE]. May Allah bless our master Muḥammad and his household and companions, and give peace."

BIBLIOGRAPHY

المَصَادِرُ وَالمَرَاجِعُ

al-Anṣārī, Zakariyā. *Asnā al-maṭālib fi sharḥ Rawḍ al-ṭālib.* n.a.: Dār al-Kitāb al-Islāmī, n.d.

al-Bukhārī, Muḥammad bin Ismā'īl Abū 'Abd Allāh. *Al-Jāmi' al-ṣaḥīḥ al-mukhtaṣar min umūr rasūli Llāh ﷺ wa sunanihi wa ayyāmihi (Ṣaḥīḥ al-Bukhārī)* ("Bukhārī"). Edited by Muḥammad Zuhayr bin Nāsir al-Nāṣir. n.a.: Dār Tawq al-Najāh, 1422AH.

al-Dumyāṭī, Abū Bakr 'Uthmān bin Muḥammad. *I'yānat al-ṭālibin.* Beirut: Dār al-Fikr, 1997/1418.

Furber, Musa. *The Accessible Conspectus.* n.a.: Islamosaic, 2015.

al-Haytamī, Aḥmed bin 'Alī bin Ḥajar. *Tuḥfat al-muhtāj sharḥ Al-Minhāj.* Beirut: Dār Iḥyā al-Turāth al-'Arabī, 1983/1357.

al-Jamal, Sulaymān bin 'Umar. *Futūḥāt al-Wahhāb.* n.a., n.d.

al-Māwardī, 'Abū al-Ḥasan 'Alī bin Muḥammad. *Al-Ḥāwī al-kabīr fī fiqh madhhab al-Imām al-Shāfi'ī.* Beirut: Dār al-Kutub al-'Ilmiyyah, 1999/1419.

Muslim bin al-Ḥajjāj. *Al-Musnad al-ṣaḥīḥ al-mukhtaṣar bi-naql al-'adl 'an al-'adl ilā rasūl Allāh* ﷺ ("Muslim"). Edited by Muḥammad Fu'ād 'Abd al-Bāqī. Beirut: Dār Iḥyā' al-Turāth, n.d.

al-Nawawī, Yaḥyā bin Sharaf. *Al-Majmū' sharḥ Al-Muhadhdhab.* Beirut: Dār al-Fikr li-l-Ṭibāh wa-l-Nashr, n.d.

———. *Rawḍat al-ṭālibīn.* Edited by Zuhary al-Shāwīsh. Beirut: Al-Maktab al-Islāmī, 1991/1412.

———. *Al-Minhāj sharḥ Ṣaḥīḥ Muslim bin al-Ḥajjāj*, 2nd ed. Beirut: Dār Iḥyā' al-Turāth, 1392AH.

al-Rāfi'ī, 'Abd al-Karīm bin Muḥammad. *Al-'Azīz sharḥ Al-Wajīz* (*Al-Sharḥ al-kabīr*). Edited by 'Alī Mu'awwiḍ and 'Ādil 'Abd al-Wujūd, 1st edition. Beirut: Dār al-Kutub al-'Ilmiyyah, 1997/1417.

———. *Al-Muḥarrar.* Edited by Muḥammad Ḥasan Ismā'īl. Beirut: Dār al-Kutub al-'Ilmiyyah, 2005.

al-Ramlī, Shams al-Dīn Muḥammad bin Abī al-'Abbās. *Nihāyat al-muḥtāj.* Beirut: Dār al-Fikr, 1984/1404.

al-Shīrāzī, Abū Isḥāq Ibrāhīm bin 'Alī. *Al-Muhadhdhab fī fiqh al-Shāfi'ī.* Beirut: Dār al-Kutub al-'Ilmiyyah, n.d.

al-Shirbīnī, Shams al-Dīn bin Aḥmad al-Khaṭīb. *Al-Iqnā'.* Beirut: Dār al-Fikr, n.d.

———. *Mughni al-muḥtāj.*Beirut: Dār al-Kutub al-'Ilmiyyah, 1994/1415.

al-Tirmidhī, Muḥammad bin 'Īsā bin Sawrah bin Mūsā. *Al-Sunan* ("Tirmidhī"). Edited by Aḥmed Muḥammad Shākir, et al, 2nd edition. Cairo: Sharikah Maktabah wa Maṭba'ah Muṣṭafā al-Bābī al-Ḥalabī, 1975/1395.

DETAILED TABLE OF CONTENTS

المُحْتَوَيَاتُ المُفَصَّلَةُ

PREFACE, IX

INTRODUCTION, 1

1 CREED, 3

What Is Required of Every Responsible Individual 3
Meaning of the Testifications of Faith 3
The First Testification 4
The Second Testification 5
Obligatory to Believe in Divine Disclosures 5
Summary of Knowing Allah Most High 6
What Is Necessary for Allah 8
What Is Impossible for Allah 10
General Proof for the Existence of Allah and His Attributes 11
Answer to Whomever Asks "What Is Allah?" 12
Summary of Knowing the Prophets (Blessings and Peace Be Upon Them) 15
What Is Necessary for the Prophets 16
What Is Impossible for the Prophets 17
What Removes a Person from Islam 19
Apostasy Via the Heart 19
Apostasy Through the Limbs 23
Apostasy Through the Tongue 24
A Principle for Knowing Many [Types] of Disbelief 29
Some of the Rulings Related to Apostates 30
What Is Required of Responsible Individuals 32

DETAILED TABLE OF CONTENTS

2 PURIFICATION AND PRAYER 34
Prayer Times 34
What Is Required of Guardians 36
Obligatory Acts of Ablution 37
Ablution Invalidators 38
What Is Required Consequent to Something Exiting the Two Waste Passages 39
The Obligatory Acts of the Purificatory Bath and What Necessitates It 40
The Conditions for Purification and the Essential Elements of Dry Ablution 41
What Is Unlawful Due to Minor And Other Ritual Impurities 42
Removing Filth 44
Other Conditions for Prayer 45
Prayer Invalidators 46
Conditions for Prayer Being Accepted 48
The Essential Elements of Prayer 49
Congregational and Friday Prayers 53
Conditions for Following 56
Funerals 58

3 ZAKAT 62
What Items Obligate Zakat 62
Livestock 63
Agriculture 64
Money 65
Trade 66
Zakat al-Fiṭr 67
Zakat Recipients 68

4 FASTING 69
Who Is Required to Fast and Who Is Allowed to Not Fast 69
Obligatory Acts of Fasting and Its Conditions 70
Unlawful Fasting 72
Intercourse in the Daytime During Ramadan 73

5 HAJJ 74
Who Is Obligated to Perform Hajj and Umrah 74
Essential Elements of Hajj and Umrah 74
What Is Unlawful to Pilgrims 75
What Becomes Obligatory due to Performing an act that is Unlawful during Pilgrimage 77

Obligatory Acts of Hajj and Umrah 77
Hunting and Foraging Within the Sacred Precincts 78

6 **TRANSACTIONS 79**
What Is Required in Transactions and Marriage 79
Forbidden Sales 81
Obligatory Support and Related Things 87

7 **PURIFICATION OF THE SELF 89**
Duties of the Heart 89
Precious Advice from a Dignified Scholar 94

8 **CLARIFYING ACTS OF DISOBEDIENCE 97**
The Heart 97
The Stomach 100
The Eyes 102
The Tongue 105
The Ears 110
The Hands 111
The Private Parts 116
The Legs 119
The Body 120
Repentance 128

This page left blank

Also from Islamosaic

Ark of Salvation

Connecting to the Quran

Etiquette with the Quran

Infamies of the Soul

Hadith Nomenclature Primers

Hanbali Acts of Worship

Ibn Juzay's Sufic Exegesis

Refutation of Those Who Do Not Follow the Four Schools

Sharḥ Al-Waraqāt

Shaykh al-Sulamī's Waṣiyyah

Supplement for the Seeker of Certitude

The Accessible Conspectus

The Encompassing Epistle

The Evident Memorandum

The Ultimate Conspectus

ISLAMOSAIC

www.islamosaic.com

www.ingramcontent.com/pod-product-compliance
Lightning Source LLC
Chambersburg PA
CBHW030332100526
44592CB00010B/665
* 9 7 8 1 9 4 4 9 0 4 1 9 7 *